Piaget
for
Educators
A Multimedia Program

Robert B. Sund

University of Northern Colorado

Charles E. Merrill Publishing Company
A Bell & Howell Company
Columbus, Ohio 43216

Published by
Charles E. Merrill Publishing Company
A Bell & Howell Company
Columbus, Ohio 43216

This book was set in Palatino.
The production editor was Sandy Smith.
The cover was designed by Will Chenoweth.

International Standard Book Number: 0-675-08589-6

Library of Congress Catalog Number: 76-4053

2 3 4 5 6 7 8 9 10—81 80 79 78 77

Printed in the United States of America

Preface

Jean Piaget has been identified as one of the great contributors to knowledge in our time. His theory of intellectual (cognitive) development is influencing school curriculum, educational materials, clinical psychology, psychiatry, learning theory, and instructional methodology. He has received numerous international awards, including the American Psychological Association Distinguished Scientific Contribution Award, and honorary degrees. Yet, most Americans remain comparatively ignorant of his work.

This is, in part, due to the difficulty in obtaining a practical, simple introduction to his theory. Piaget is a researcher. His writings mainly are reports of his research and are written in scholarly style. Although this is essential to insure accuracy in communication and acceptance by the academic community, it makes it difficult for the reader to grasp the essence or the significance of his theory. In talking to parents and teachers about Piaget's theory, I have seen that they are eager to read more about it. Often they ask, "What can I read that wouldn't be too difficult and academic?" I have referred them to one of the several books presently on the market. Their reactions to these often have been mixed. Because of this and for other reasons, I have intended, since returning from Geneva in 1964, to produce a simple, readable introduction to Piaget's theory.

This media program is the product of that effort. It is intended specifically to introduce parents, psychologists, counselors, religious leaders, and educators to the theory. The text, films, and tapes reinforce each other to this end. They are not meant to give an extensive coverage of the area of cognitive development because there are several books that already do this well.

There is a danger in trying to simplify something as complex as Piaget's theory. This is especially true since the theory has evolved for close to fifty years, and, even today, Piaget and his coworkers are busy making minor alterations to it. Hopefully, however, this media program will be the first step toward learning about Piaget, and further reading will supplement any points that need additional clarification.

I have endeavored to make the text practical and easy reading by using diagrams and summary lists to clarify the main ideas and by avoiding extensive quotations or documentation. The characteristics of each stage of development are presented in separate chapters. General implications of Piaget's work and specific suggestions for teaching are discussed in other chapters. These suggestions should help you apply the theory in a learning environment and become more aware of the breadth and significance of Piaget's work. The true test of the value of these ideas, however, will come as you apply them and judge whether they help you interact more effectively with children. Self-evaluation Inventories are provided in various parts of the book as guides to check how well you have learned some of the basic concepts of Piaget's theory. *Begin reading the text and follow the directions for using the MEDIAPAK audio-visual components.*

Over the years, several hundred teachers and parents throughout this country have been trained by me to interview children in order to gain insights into their cognitive abilities. Administering these interviews usually results in what I call "Piagetian Shock." To most people, reading about the theory is just an intellectual exercise, but this changes when they sit down with a child and evaluate his thinking using Piagetian tasks. The interviewers are always amazed by what children intellectually do. *The giving of interviews is truly an exciting experience.* For this reason, suggestions for administering interviews for most of Piaget's levels are listed. Each interviewing task is followed by an explanation of what is involved in its interpretation. Caution should be noted here. The purpose of these interviews is not to prepare you as a clinical or research psychologist but merely to reinforce how children cognitively vary.

Listed at the end of the text is a brief description of excellent films, filmstrips, and audio cassette tapes explaining Piaget's theory. These are well worth the time and effort to see and hear. Some paper-and-pencil tests are also included for the concrete-operational and formal-operational levels to show in a different way the types of tasks individuals at these levels should be able to perform.

For those who want to reinforce and apply what they learn from this program, it is suggested that they read R. M. Gorman, *Discovering Piaget: A Guide for Teachers,* (Merrill, 1972). It is written in a semi-programmed style, giving the reader many opportunities to interpret what a child is doing cognitively and then explaining in considerable detail the child's thinking.

I am deeply indebted to Dr. David Elkind who convinced me to go to Geneva in 1964; to Dr. Piaget for the privilege of hearing him lecture and discuss research; to Dr. Barbel Inhelder who made the arrangements for me to attend the Piaget lectures, discussions, and faculty meetings of the institute, observe the interviewing of children, attend her classes, and meet with her on occasion in spite of her taxing schedule; to Dr. Gert Morgenstern, a visiting fellow from Montreal at the institute, who was helpful in explaining many points about Piaget's work and who read and edited my first effort in writing about his theory while I was in Geneva in 1964; to Dr. John Flavell for his extensive review of Piaget's research (I have used it frequently and am constantly amazed at the comprehensiveness of his book; and to many of my colleagues, who have encouraged my effort, specifically the many who have been involved in training teachers in Piagetian theory and testing much of the material in this book: Rodger Bybee, Alan McCormack, James McClurg, Ken Olson, Leslie Trowbridge, George Crockett, Jay Hackett, Don Adams, John Hunt, Bill Tillery, Chet Ruan, and Don Acheson.

Special gratitude goes to the doctoral candidates with whom I associated in carrying on Piagetian research: Dan Ball, Steve Sayre, Paul Ankney, Lyle Joyce, Bill Gurney, Sandra Bowland, Don Carlson, Tim Cooney, and James Fournier.

Piaget has influenced me considerably in better understanding myself and the characteristics of a good learning environment, in perceiving children, and in interacting socially and intellectually with others on a path toward greater humanness. It has been a continual growth experience since my first encounter with David Elkind when he opened my thoughts to cognitive development. I hope the same will happen for you as you penetrate the significance of Piaget's work in this book and the accompanying media.

Contents

Appendixes

Piaget and His Work 1

Jean Piaget is a model of a truly exciting person. Donald B. Robinson, in his book *100 Most Important People in the World Today*, lists Piaget. Having had an opportunity to attend the Jean Jacques Rousseau Institute's faculty discussions headed by Piaget, I soon realized he is a man of great wisdom.[1] At the institute in Geneva, Switzerland, where Piaget still continues research, he attracts scholars from around the world who wish to review their theories and research with him. He encourages such research in a breadth of areas. The institute itself has a staff of people competent in various fields, such as psychology, psychiatry, mathematics, and philosophy. How did Piaget become a man fostering the integration of diverse academic disciplines in the pursuit of knowledge? For an answer to this question, one has to look at his background.

Background

Piaget was born in Neuchatel, Switzerland, just before the turn of the century (August 9, 1896). His father was a scholar of medieval history and his mother was an intelligent person, although fraught with neurotic tendencies. His mother's poor mental health made his home life somewhat unpleasant. Therefore, early in his youth Piaget sought satisfaction away from home. He became fascinated with nature. At age ten he wrote a paper on the albino sparrow which was published in a natural history journal. Later, he asked the director of the Neuchatel natural history museum, Paul Godet, if he could help him after school. Godet put him to work labeling mollusks and, after each session, would give Piaget a number of classified rare specimens for his own collection.

Piaget worked for four years labeling and studying the museum mollusk collections. He felt competent enough, by the time of Godet's death in 1911, to

---

[1] The institute is now in a new residence, l'Ecole de Psychologie des Sciences de l'Education.

write papers on the subject and, subsequently, was offered a position in the natural history museum in Geneva when he was fifteen. Although flattered by this offer, he rejected it so that he could continue his studies in secondary school for two more years.

Piaget's biological interest was tempered by his godfather, Samuel Cornut, a Swiss scholar. Cornut introduced him to philosophy, causing him to become particularly interested in epistemology or how individuals come to know what they do. How does the individual grow and become a philosophical being capable of logic and reason? What is knowledge? How do we attain it? Is the way to true knowledge through the senses, as the pragmatists believe, or through the use of our minds? How has knowledge changed with man's evolution? What are the biological explanations of knowledge? Questions like these were to play a major role during Piaget's adult years in his formulation of the theory of cognitive development.

Piaget finished his first degree at the University of Neuchatel at the age of twenty. He obtained his doctorate at that institution at the age of twenty-two, doing a dissertation on mollusks. His interest in psychology was stimulated by his mother's poor mental health; so he went after graduation in 1918 to the University of Zurich in Switzerland to study psychology. In Zurich he worked in several psychological laboratories and in a psychiatric clinic. In 1919, dissatisfied with the research going on in Zurich, he left to study at the Sorbonne in Paris. In 1920 he was recommended to Theophile Simon who had previously helped Alfred Binet construct the first intelligence test. Simon invited Piaget to use the Binet Laboratory facilities in Paris to develop a French standardized test of Burt's reasoning test. Piaget accepted this invitation. Through his investigations, he became very interested in the types of wrong answers children gave for some of the items on the test. He began to investigate the problem by using clinical-psychological questioning techniques rather than traditional scientific experimental methods. As a result of these early studies, Piaget discovered that children often experience difficulties with tasks involving the inclusion of parts with wholes, coordination of relations, and classification. It surprised him that this was so with some children even up to age twelve. He followed these preliminary studies with two years of investigations of the verbal reasoning of normal and abnormal children. This research confirmed to Piaget that logic was not inborn and that the *clinical method* could be used to determine the sequence of a child's development. Piaget's interest was kindled, and his research directed his intellect for much of his life to come.

In 1921 Piaget accepted a position as director of research of the Jean Jacques Rousseau Institute. This position allowed him considerable freedom in investigating children's thinking. He continued to use the clinical approach by presenting children at various age levels with tasks requiring manipulation of objects and noting how they responded. He and his wife, a former student, also devoted several years to observing their three children. These observations, plus clinical research, became the basis for numerous books and articles on child development.

His early publications established Piaget as an authority on child development and encouraged a significant following in this country during the 1920s and

1930s. However, largely due to the ascendancy of other psychologies in the United States and the lack of English translations of his works, interest in his theory diminished. During the 1940s, five of his books were translated, and a renewed interest in his work emerged throughout the world. Finally in 1942, in *The Psychology of Intelligence*, Piaget outlined for the first time the foundation of his theory of mental (cognitive) development.

Other Influences on His Work

Other influences, besides his research, affected Piaget's later work. One was his appointment in 1929 as professor of history of scientific thought at the University of Geneva, a position he held until 1939. In this position, Piaget focused on investigating children's scientific concepts. Albert Einstein, in a discussion with Piaget in the early 1940s, suggested that he study children's concepts of time, velocity, and movement. Piaget followed this advice and eventually summarized research on these subjects in several books.

In 1947, in recognition of his international scholarly prominence, Piaget was appointed head of the Swiss delegation to UNESCO. From 1952 to 1962, he was professor of genetic psychology at the University of Paris. His main duties, however, were still with the Jean Jacques Rousseau Institute which became a part of the University of Geneva during this period. In 1956, Piaget created the International Center for Genetic Epistemology within the faculty of science at the University of Geneva. The purpose of this institute is to encourage faculty from various disciplines and parts of the world to work on a problem related to cognition, how humans come to know what they know. Each member involved in the institute brings his own experience to a research problem under study. The ideas from these various specialists are integrated through faculty discussions, and the end result of their work is a publication, a monograph, on the topic. The institute has already published several monographs related to thinking and the learning process.

Continued Importance

Although Piaget is in his late seventies, he continues to investigate how man comes to know what he knows, to direct research, and to write. His acclaim and international recognition continues among psychologists, philosophers, and educators. He has become a model of what Abraham Maslow calls a "self-actualized man." His name, like Freud, will forever be imprinted in the annuals of man's history as one who penetrated further into the essence of human development.

Piaget's Theory
of Cognitive
Development 2

Psychological Adaptation

Our modern view of the human species is in a state of tremendous change because of changing conceptualizations of mentality, development, consciousness, brain function, creativity, contentment, and mental health. The wealth of present discoveries in psychology, sociology, anthropology, and other behavioral sciences contributes to our realization that a human is truly a complex and marvelous creature with fantastic potential. These revelations give us hope because problems of great complexity confront us daily, requiring superior humans.

Charles Darwin explained how species evolve. His theory of natural selection stresses the importance of anatomical and physiological fitness. Our times, however, require the application of psychological factors as well to this theory. The importance of psychological aspects of survival has been stressed by many of our contemporary authors. For example, Alvin Toffler, in his book, *Future Shock*, hypothesizes that, because of modern developments, a selective factor operating in determining human survival is change. Humans must come to understand change, accept it, and be prepared for it at an accelerating rate.

Many animal behaviorists give credence to the influence of psychological factors in natural selection. Jane van Lawick-Goodall, studying chimpanzees in the Gombe Stream Chimpanzee Reserve in Tanzania, revealed the importance of these factors in chimp survival. She found, for example, that the death of a chimp affects the other individuals in the colony. When death occurs the members go through a period of mourning, the intensity of which may cause some to die, as is sometimes the case with humans. Goodall's research further reveals the importance of such human-like behaviors as touching, grooming, sleeping protectively with another, caressing, game playing, etc. She suggests that chimpanzees often demonstrate these behaviors to a higher degree than humans. Other animal behaviorists have observed the development of status hierarchies among animals, for example, the pecking order of chickens and leaders in wolf colonies.

Maslow, in studying individuals with healthy personalities, found they were very active, committed to something they believed in, creative, and possessed a high self-esteem. How can people be helped to achieve a positive self-concept? The answer is complex. One contributing factor, however, is the development of the intellect. It is through intellectual resources that the individual is able to resolve problems. Piaget and his coworkers offer guidance on how the intellect can be developed.

The Stages of Cognitive Development

Through fifty years of extensive investigations of the thinking behavior of children, Piaget has slowly evolved a theory of cognitive development. Cognition involves the intellectual activities of the mind including: remembering, evoking, perceiving, imagining, and abstracting.

Just as Freud pointed out that individuals go through several stages of sexual development, Piaget has found that they also evolve through increasingly complex phases of mental development. A child of two differs cognitively in what she is able to perform from a four year old; a four year old differs from a child of seven, etc. Piaget outlines four major periods of mental development. Some of these, however, have several phases. These stage should not be thought of as static. Rather, the child should be looked at as progressing through them in a continuous mental development. Each day, the child's mind grows in its capacity to interact with the environment. Sufficient maturation and appropriate experiences enable her to develop mental structures for better handling stimuli from her surroundings. Piaget believes the mind develops certain strategies and that these evolve in a rather progressive way as the child matures. It is the progressive differences of these mental structures that characterize each of the four stages, the sequence of which is listed below:

Sensory-Motor	0–2 years
Preoperational	2–7 years
Concrete-Operational	7–11 years
Formal-Operational	11–14 years

The year designations assigned to the levels indicate the length of the periods of each stage and were determined with French-Swiss children. There has been some research to indicate, and Piaget has stated, that the mean attainment of the levels above may vary. He says:

> However, the order of succession has shown itself to be constant—as each stage is necessary to the construction of the following one—the average age at which children go through each stage can vary considerably from one social environment to another, or from one country or even region within a country to another.[1]

---

[1] Jean Piaget, "Intellectual Evolution from Adolescence to Adulthood," Third International Convention and Awarding of Foneme Prizes, Milan, May 9–10, 1970, Foneme Foundation, p. 161.

The stages should only be thought of as helpful labels for the educator, parent, or theorist to characterize the mental progression of children. Knowing Piaget's stage characteristics helps the individual predict what a group of children will be able to do cognitively. However, identifying stages and using them as a guide should in no way lessen the understanding of the continuity of cognitive development of the individual. Children often are in transition from one stage to another. Therefore, a child may not exactly pass from the sensory-motor level to preoperational level at age two, although the majority of children will fall within the periods indicated.

Influences on Cognitive Development

Maturation and Experience

It is obvious that as a child lives he grows and develops. There are in the maturation process physiological and anatomical changes which contribute to the cognitive development of the person.

As a baby matures physically, she moves, crawls, and investigates her environment. When she encounters something in the environment, for example, a rattle, she confronts a stimulus. She may move and shake it. When a child performs actions on a stimulus, she acquires physical experience and learns that she can interact with objects in her environment. Piaget believes physical action enables the child to later develop mental action. That is, she eventually is capable of transferring physical action into thought. For this reason, Piaget says, "There is no learning without experience." And to Piaget, physical action is a basic component of experience.

Piaget divides experience into two parts: physical and logical-mathematical. Physical experience occurs when children physically act on objects in the environment. In the process of doing this they eventually recognize that there is more involved in acting on objects than just physical activity. For example, they realize that objects may be ordered from short to long. In other words, children, from having physical experiences, eventually have logical-mathematical experiences. These logical-mathematical experiences contribute to the formation of structures in the mind that the child can call upon in the future.

Social Experience

Social experience contributes to intelligence because, through social interaction, individuals are forced to consider others' views of the world and to develop language competency. For example, the young child of three or four thinks the way she perceives things is the way all individuals perceive them. Try playing a game with a three year old, and you will see how egocentric she is; she won't follow rules unless they coincide with her perception of the game. As children interact with other humans, they slowly realize phenomena may be perceived in various ways. Through language and its use in argument, a child gains mental experience enabling and sometimes forcing her mind to develop new operations or techniques for perceiving and solving problems. Social experience also serves as the basis through which a child becomes less egocentric and develops certain mental concepts not having physical referents, such as humility, honesty, and other ethical beliefs.

Equilibration

Humans, like other living creatures, biologically exhibit a tendency to organize processes into integrated systems. For example, an infant moves her fingers in diverse ways. Slowly, she integrates their motion into the ability to grasp. Piaget would say that the child has constructed in her mind a grasping structure which she can use in the future whenever she wishes. The child mentally has adapted to a stimulus, something to be grasped, and has changed as a result.

Why does an individual take in information and mentally adapt to the environment? Why does she develop mental systems for handling information to be retrieved and used in various ways later in life? Piaget suggests that an equilibration process is the mental counterpart of physically adapting to the environment. He believes it is human nature to be in a state of equilibrium. However, disequilibrium may occur when an individual interacts with a stimulus. She responds and, as a result, returns to a state of equilibrium. Piaget calls this process of an individual's mentally reacting to stimuli to attain equilibrium *equilibration*. It is an internal, self-regulating mental process by which individuals continually change and develop.

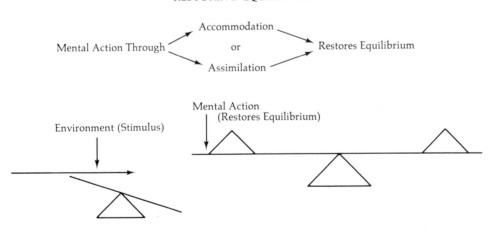

EQUILIBRATION—THE PROCESS OF
RESTORING EQUILIBRIUM

Accommodation

Mental Action Through   or   Restores Equilibrium

Assimilation

Mental Action
(Restores Equilibrium)

Environment (Stimulus)

Piaget breaks equilibration into two categories, assimilation and accommodation.

1. *Assimilation* involves taking in information from the environment and incorporating it into existing mental schemes or structures.
2. *Accommodation* involves the modification or fabrication of mental schemes and structures.

These processes may be understood somewhat simply by thinking of the mind as if it were a file cabinet. As the mind encounters information, it files it or *assimilates* it. When the information becomes part of the file and changes its contents, it is *accommodated*. When a baby experiences several different chairs and eventually mentally constitutes the concept *chair*, she has accommodated information because a new scheme was formulated for handling this concept.[2] You might think of the assimilation process as acting on and taking in information and the accommodation process as utilizing this information to modify existing mental schemes or construct new ones.

Admittedly, the above description of the equilibration process is somewhat simplistic. A human interacting with his environment may be assimilating and accommodating simultaneously. For example, a child sees a large object and, after thinking, realizes it is a table. She has assimilated the information. However, on closer observation, the child realizes the object differs considerably from her concept of a table—it has drawers. She realizes, or accommodates, that it is some kind of work area. She may not as yet have a name for the object (desk), but because she has accommodated she knows this table's function differs from that of an ordinary dining table.

Schemes, or the products of the equilibrium process, are those actions the mind retains that are *repeatable and generalizable*. They are what is common

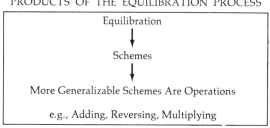

PRODUCTS OF THE EQUILIBRATION PROCESS

Equilibration

↓

Schemes

↓

More Generalizable Schemes Are Operations

e.g., Adding, Reversing, Multiplying

about similar actions carried out at different times, for example, *putting* a rattle on a blanket, *putting* candy on a blanket, *putting* any object on a blanket. Therefore they include the general structuring of actions and operations. As a child develops, the schemes are organized into higher-order mental structures called operations, e.g., adding, classifying, and conserving mass. Just as body structures adapt and change as they interact with the environment, e.g., the arm muscles enlarge with exertion over a period of time, so do mental structures—the schemes. Because of this adaptation, the individual progressively demonstrates more rational interaction.

To Piaget, then, intelligence evolves and develops as life continues. The factors of maturation, social and physical experience, and equilibration each play

---

[2] Schemes are general mental patterns or organized patterns of behavior, e.g., holding a glass and bringing it to the mouth to drink. Unfortunately, Piaget has used in his later publications both the word *scheme* and *schema*, and this has led to confusion. In this book, scheme is defined as above. For a clearer definition to these words see Hermine Sinclair, "Representation and Memory," in *Piagetian Cognitive Development Research and Mathematical Education* (Washington, D.C.: National Council of Teachers of Mathematics), p. 133.

a role in the individual's progression through the stages of cognitive development. However, the degree to which each of these factors manifests itself varies greatly with individuals, causing a wide diversity among them.

Often when people are introduced to Piaget's theory, they are overwhelmed by its complexity. This, in part, is due to the failure of writers to give a generalized overview of the stages before going into depth with each level. For this reason, a brief summary of the stages follows. It is suggested that you spend considerable time thinking about this information before progressing to the other chapters so as to better grasp how different aspects of each of the levels relate to the theory.

General Description of Piaget's Stages

The Sensory-Motor Stage: 0–2 Years

(A Period of Discriminating and Labeling)

The sensory-motor stage is so named because the child mainly interacts with the environment through her senses and muscles and is directed by stimuli from without. At birth, the infant is limited to using reflexes, such as sucking, crying, and grasping. Her movements are initially erratic. She develops her ability to perceive, touch, move, etc., during this stage. As the child interacts with her surroundings, she slowly learns to handle it better. For example, opportunities to interact with her environment improve her perception from seeing things as only flat to seeing them as having depth and dimension. In the early part of this stage (up to almost nine months) the concept of *object permanence* has not developed. That is, the child does not realize that an object still exists even when out of sight. Therefore, she is limited to dealing with external stimuli rather than mental pictures of them. An infant will not search for an object hidden from her immediate view. An object not directly perceived does not exist for her.

The sensory-motor child is concerned with organizing and coordinating physical actions. Piaget believes this involvement with physical actions serves as the basis for the development of mental actions later in the period. For example, a child of one to four months has a "hands-to-mouth orientation," that is, whenever she is given an object, she places it in her mouth. Children of eight to twelve months, however, are more selective of what they place in their mouths and are more likely to demonstrate means-end behavior. A child of one to four months may pull a blanket because of the pleasure she gets from grasping and feeling it. If a parent places toys, sweets, etc., on the blanket, the child may or may not pull the blanket toward her. Around eight months, however, the child may demonstrate means-end intelligence by purposefully pulling a blanket toward her to achieve her goal of obtaining the objects on the blanket.

Early possibilities for acting on objects make it possible during the eight to twelve month period for the child to mentally develop means-end ability. Thousands of actions made on objects also eventually enable the child to differentiate herself from other objects, thereby beginning the conceptualization of her identity as separate from the surrounding environment. Subsequently, by nine months, most children conceive of *object permanence*, that is, the existence of an object even though it may be outside the child's perceptual field. By the end of this period, a child has developed representational thought, that is, the ability to represent an object in the mind. She will, for example, be able to locate an object even though it is placed first under one then another and another pillow and hidden from view. In summary, in the two years of the sensory-motor period, the child makes tremendous gains in evolving toward intelligent behavior. Verbally, however, the sensory-motor child does not progress very much, except that she can name objects.

The Preoperational Stage: 2–7 Years

(Intuitive, Stimulus-limited Period)

Preoperational thought spans approximately ages two through seven years, thus including most children in kindergarten, first grade, and second grade. Though a child in this stage can form mental representations and label them verbally, she has not yet developed the ability to carry out mental transformations called *operations*. Operations include abilities, such as to simultaneously think about more than one aspect of a problem, order a series of events, and understand that the quantity, weight, and volume of matter are conserved under ordinary conditions even though something may alter in appearance.

For example, a preoperational child is confused by the following conservation task. Two glasses are placed in front of her. One is tall and filled with colored water, and the other is short, larger in diameter, and empty. All of the colored water from the tall glass is poured into the short glass. The child is asked, "Is there more, less, or the same amount of colored water in the small glass as there was in the large glass?" Preoperational children usually respond by saying, "There is more in the tall glass." The interviewer may ask, "Was there any water added or taken away from the glasses?" The child will say, "No." The child's statement is repeated, "But you think there is more water in the tall glass?" Again the child will say, "Yes." The child responds in apparently illogical manner because she does not as yet realize that rearranging matter does not affect the amount of material present. Most mathematical activities, such as adding, subtracting, and multiplying are operations. Because preoperational children are unable to perform operational functions, they appear illogical to adults.

During this stage the child is also highly egocentric. She finds it difficult to comprehend views other than her own. She does not understand chance and probability because she assumes only one truth or one event is possible in any given situation. She often gives anthropomorphic explanations for observed natural events. That is, she gives human qualities to nonhuman entities. For example, she might explain a plant's bending toward a window as it "likes light" or it "wants to."

During the latter part of this stage, memory further develops so that the child has the ability to think of past and future, but she is limited in how far she goes in either direction.

The Concrete-Operational Stage: 7–11 Years

(Performing Operations Period)

Between seven and eleven years of age, the child develops the ability to perform mental operations. Following a set of logical rules, her mental processes are incorporated into coherent systems. The operations are called *concrete* because they are usually carried out with actual objects. For example, when a child is given a piece of clay to roll out, she is mentally aware that the amount of clay has not been changed by manipulating it. She can also *think* of forming the clay back to the way it was. In other words, she is capable of reversing her thought process. However, if presented with a problem of changing the form of clay in abstract terms without actually modifying it, the child may experience difficulties.

Problems involving conservation of quantity, weight, and volume are solved by these children at the end of this stage, and they can satisfactorily justify their solutions. Concrete-operational children can also consider two dimensions of a problem simultaneously. Changing events can be *ordered* by them into a chronological sequence. They observe, judge, and evaluate in less egocentric terms and formulate more objective explanations than children in the lower stages. However, they still experience difficulty in expressing hypotheses or in following a series of related ideas, particularly if concrete referents are not available.

The Formal-Operational Stage: 11–14 Years

(Propositional Thinking Period)

Between twelve and fifteen years of age, children begin to function intellectually as adults. This stage marks the child's emancipation from dependence on direct perception of objects. In contrast to the concrete-operational child, the adolescent thinker can represent her own thoughts by symbols, consider ideals as opposed to realities, form inferences based on stated sets of assumptions (propositional thinking), formulate complex and abstract theories, and reflect upon her thought processes (reflexive thinking). The formal-operational adolescent can carry out mental experiments as well as actual ones, and she understands probability. In short, the kind of cognition that is considered adult is now the rule rather than the exception.

Summary of Piaget's Stages of Mental Development

SENSORY-MOTOR   Birth–2 Years

1. Direction by stimuli, outside the mind
2. Preverbal stage, no language except names
3. Thought proceeding from actions
4. Perception and identification of objects
5. By end of period, ability to distinguish among parents, animals
6. Rudimentary sense of direction and purpose late in stage

7. Present time
8. Immediate space
9. Representational thought—mentally represents objects

PREOPERATIONAL   2–7 Years

1. No performance of operations but development of language
2. No abstract thinking
3. Egocentrism
4. Nonreversible thinking
5. Action on perceptive impulses
6. Static thought, no series of operations
7. Time, present, future, past thought; of short duration
8. Space, house, yard, neighborhood

CONCRETE-OPERATIONAL   7–11 Years

1. Performance of operations; combining, separating, ordering, seriating, multiplying or repeating, dividing, substituting, reversible thinking, one-to-one correspondence by end of period, analyzing, classifying, measuring

FORMAL-OPERATIONAL   11–14 Years

1. Hypothetical-deductive thinking
2. Propositional thinking, thinking about thinking
3. Reflexive thinking
4. Synthesizing, relating large bodies of information and creating new and unique thoughts
5. Imagining, e.g., idealistic or utopian societies
6. Abstract, nonconcrete conceptual thinking
7. Understanding of probability
8. Questioning ethics and values
9. Formulating of theories
10. Broadening of time concept to infinity
11. Space, conception of the universe and molecular space

Summary

Modern science increasingly reveals the complexity of man in the development of emotions and intellect. Piaget has studied for more than fifty years the cognitive development of man. He concludes from his research that the individual passes through four main stages of cognitive development in the maturation process: 1) sensory-motor—0–2 years, 2) preoperational—2–7 years, 3) concrete-operational—7–11 years, and 4) formal-operational—11–14 years. Four factors influence the progression through these levels: 1) maturation, 2) physical experience, 3) social experience, and 4) equilibration.

When an individual encounters something in her environment and acts on it, she mentally equilibrates. Equilibration is a mental, self-regulating process consisting of assimilation and accommodation. Assimilation involves absorbing information and incorporating it into mental schemes. Accommodation is the process of fabricating or modifying existing mental schemes. The schemes produced as a result of equilibration are general mental or organized patterns that the mind is capable of manifesting when the environment or the will demands.

Each stage of cognitive development is characterized by the ability to perform certain functions. Progression through the stages is always in the sequence outlined, but some individuals never reach the higher levels of cognitive development.

Go to the first MEDIAPAK audio-visual component in this program, MEDIAPAK A. When you have completed it, return to this text and take the Self-evaluation Inventory on page 14.

Self-evaluation Inventory

Directions: Listed below are some of the main topics covered in Chapters 1 and 2 and MEDIAPAK A. Read each statement and rate it on the scale TWICE: once according to what you knew about the topic before starting this part of the program and again according to what you've learned after completing it. Circle the appropriate number and mark B for before and A for after next to the number as indicated below.

Topic	Student Evaluation					
	Low		Moderate		High	
Example: Distinguish among important Piagetian mental operations	①B	2	3	4	5	⑥A
1. The Jean Jacques Rousseau Institute	1	2	3	4	5	6
2. Piaget's life	1	2	3	4	5	6
3. How Piaget became involved in his life work	1	2	3	4	5	6
4. The names of Piaget's four stages and their age spans	1	2	3	4	5	6
5. The four factors contributing to intelligence	1	2	3	4	5	6
6. Accommodation	1	2	3	4	5	6
7. Assimilation	1	2	3	4	5	6
8. Equilibration	1	2	3	4	5	6
9. Schemes	1	2	3	4	5	6
10. Operations	1	2	3	4	5	6
11. Reversible thinking	1	2	3	4	5	6

Topic	Student Evaluation					
	Low		*Moderate*		*High*	
12. Basic characteristics of and why it is called sensory-motor stage	1	2	3	4	5	6
13. Basic characteristics of and why it is called preoperational stage	1	2	3	4	5	6
14. Basic characteristics of and why it is called concrete-operational stage	1	2	3	4	5	6
15. Basic characteristics of and why it is called the formal-operational stage	1	2	3	4	5	6
16. Cognitive development	1	2	3	4	5	6
17. How children's minds vary from those of adults	1	2	3	4	5	6

Now that you have assessed your growth after reading Chapters 1 and 2 and viewing MEDIAPAK A, review those areas above where you indicate there is either a lack of growth or confidence about the topic. Then continue with Chapter 3.

The Sensory-Motor Period: 0-2 Years 3

The first stage of mental development is the sensory-motor period. It is called this because a child, as an active organism, interacts with the environment through his senses and muscles. Humans are born with certain reflexes, such as suckling and grasping. As a baby moves about, he encounters stimuli which activate these reflexes. His behavior, however, tends to be global at first in the sense that, when the infant responds, he may be using several reflexes rather than just isolated ones.

As the child encounters the environment, he slowly begins the assimilation-accommodation process. He increasingly senses stimuli (sensory reaction) and responds to them by moving his muscles (motor reaction). For example, a two-month-old baby girl may see a rattle and become aware of its existence. She tries to reach it. At first, she has difficulty touching it. Her little hand stabs out from her body but misses the target. Her arm moves awkwardly until finally her hand feels the rattle. Slowly, by interacting with objects, the child mentally evolves techniques to better organize muscular actions so that she can eventually hit a target the first time. When she feels the rattle, many sensations enter her mind. By having numerous, similar physical experiences, she slowly begins to organize her grasping ability. In a sense, she is building basic programs for her mind. Eventually, mental actions are coordinated enabling her to conceptualize physical properties, e.g., hardness, softness, and plasticity. Later she may use this awareness of properties of an object to solve simple problems, e.g., breaking a cracker so she can eat it. Toward the end of this period she may indicate *property awareness* by saying such things as hot, cold, and broken.

Intelligent Behavior Evolves

Piaget believes that physical activity contributes to the development of intelligence. The infant's adapting his reflexes to objects around him enables him to eventually learn to perceive and discriminate. For example, when first born, an

16

infant is incapable of differentiating a woman's nipple from the skin around it. By encountering the breast area through touch and vision he soon assimilates and accommodates this difference. A four-month-old baby looks longer at a picture of a human face than at a nonsense diagram, indicating increased perceptual activity. The more discriminating perceptions a baby makes, the better his chances are later to manifest good concept development.

Parents are prone to identify intelligent behavior in their progeny and, as a result, make certain assumptions that may not be valid particularly in the early part of this period. For example, they might see their infant move a toy drum to strike it and think that he is acting in an intelligent manner. However, the infant probably moves the drum only because he is stimulated by it. It is not until the middle of this stage, (eight to twelve months) that the child imagines the consequences of an act before carrying it out. For now, the infant cannot perform an act mentally without performing it physically. If he were truly intelligent, he should be able to think in the following manner:

"I want to hit the drum but it is too far away.
If I move it closer I shall be able to hit it more easily.
Therefore, I shall move it and hit it."

The infant is not capable as yet of making his mind perform these operations. He does not have the necessary thought patterns: *If* this is done *then* this will follow. Furthermore, the sensory-motor child cannot add, group objects, classify, or perform any other similar mental operations. His world is restricted essentially to practical interaction with objects within his immediate environment which are linked to physical satisfaction. Time for him is now. He neither thinks of the past nor the future. Space involves only that which surrounds him and is limited to the area in which he acts. He has little understanding of the space included in his home or yard. This gradually changes as he becomes more involved with activities relating to space and time. The young infant is confused about the difference between himself and the world around him. By twelve months, however, he differentiates between self and other objects. For example, he may bang objects hard against a wall but not do the same thing using parts of his body.

Increasingly, as the child experiences, he begins to understand that he may control his actions. When an infant, he may cry because of discomfort or be stimulated to cry by hearing another baby. As he gets older, however, he realizes that crying may satisfy some goal. By so doing, he has learned to differentiate *means and goals*, demonstrating intelligent behavior. For example, a baby may cry when being restrained by his mother from getting into the pots and pans cupboard. He may not be experiencing physical discomfort by such restraint but may realize by crying needs are satisfied. This does not suggest that he performs a series of mental operations, such as "I want to get into the cupboard; mother is holding me back; therefore, I shall cry." Not at all. The child only knows that he cannot get the pans. If he cries he might get satisfaction, maybe not the cupboards but attention from his mother. Often mothers aware of such behavior give the child attention by picking him up or using some distraction to modify his response. How many times have you seen a mother divert the interest of a child from crying or doing something she did not want him to do? She can accomplish this because the sensory-motor child is easily diverted from his original goal.

Although intelligent behavior is evolving, behavior, at this point, is pre-verbal. Also, in a sense, the infant is *bound by the stimuli* about him rather than being able to originate them from his brain. However, even in the first months of life, the child does demonstrate some inner stimulation as seen when he originates suckling even though there is nothing present to nurse.

Stages of the Sensory-Motor Period

Piaget and his wife spent considerable time observing their three children pro-gress through this period. They concluded that a child passes through six stages of development in the sensory-motor period. The development progresses in a definite sequence, but the age attainment of each level may vary considerably from child to child. The ages given, therefore, should be considered only ap-proximations.

Six Developmental Stages—Sensory-Motor Period

1. *Stage One—0–1 month*
   Innate reflexes begin to function. The child does not just react to external stimuli.

2. *Stage Two—1–4 months*
   Primary circular (repeatable) reactions involved with the infant's body develop. Actions are nonpurposeful and repetitive for their own sake, for example, thumb sucking and fingering blankets. From here on there is increasing intentionality of the child, and means-end relations begin to occur.

3. *Stage Three—4–8 months*
   Secondary circular (repetitive) actions develop. Now the child manipulates objects, for example, pulls toys toward him. These are secondary reactions since these objects are not of the body. Actions are no longer repeated for their own sake but because of the interesting stimuli they develop. For example, a child hits a hanging toy in his crib several times, demonstrating his ability to apply a scheme—hitting a toy.

4. *Stage Four—8–12 months*
   Object permanence is established but not completed. Self and world are not differ-entiated.

5. *Stage Five—12–18 months*
   Tertiary circular reactions develop. The child explores his environment by trial and error. In experimenting, the child is interested in novelty for its own sake.

6. *Stage Six—18–24 months*
   The transition from overt to covert representation occurs. The child can reproduce from memory and use mental symbols to refer to objects not present, for example, dog, mommy, daddy. He realizes the existence of objects not present.

Progression to Object Permanence

As the sensory-motor child progresses through this stage of development, he begins to center more on what is happening about him and increasingly pays more attention to events. Slowly, he manifests *object permanence*. That is, he comes to realize that objects continue to exist even when not in his perceptual field. The development of this process is outlined below:

Six Developmental Stages—Object Permanence

1. *Stage One—0–1 month*
   The child does not differentiate objects from self. He looks at an object only while it is in his field of vision.

2. *Stage Two—1–4 months*
   He still does not differentiate between object and self but follows an object and continues to look at the point where it has been even though it disappeared. A child of this period clearly demonstrates the role of experience in development. For example, he will search for his bottle if the nipple is exposed, but, if the bottom of the bottle is slightly shown to him from beneath the covers, the infant will not attempt to uncover it to find the nipple. He has developed some object comprehension about the nipple but not the bottom of the bottle. The child also begins to develop a coherence of various senses. Unlike in the first stage, when hearing a noise, the infant is not just startled but coordinates his hearing with seeing and looking toward the source. The infant thereby begins to discover that sound comes from certain objects.

3. *Stage Three—4–8 months*
   The child searches for objects that vanished from his grasp. He moves objects away from his face so that he can see. He also anticipates where a moving or falling object will be. The child will search for a partially hidden object (for example, a toy) but will not search for a completely hidden object.

4. *Stage Four—8–12 months*
   He searches actively for completely hidden objects. If an object is moved from one hidden place to another in front of him, the infant looks for it in the first place.

5. *Stage Five—12–18 months*
   The child realizes an object remains the same even though visibly it appears different because of distance from it. He searches for an object where he last saw it rather than going to the place where it was first hidden. However, if the infant has to infer where an object should be (for example, if it is passed behind a screen), he may start to look for it in the first hidden place.

6. *Stage Six—18 months*
   The child achieves object permanence; he realizes that objects exist separated from self and that they may move in space.

An understanding of the object permanence sequence establishes a relatively good basis for comprehending the child's evolution through this period. It should be further noted that, until and including stage three (four to eight months) of the sensory-motor period, the child has only a rudimentary sense of direction and purpose. He cannot move an object without forgetting where he placed it. He may, for example, see his father dangling keys and be stimulated by their glitter and noise. The father slyly places them under the newspaper. The child heads for the father, but once he reaches him, and the keys are no longer present, he may crawl to some other part of the room even though he saw his father place and leave the key under the newspaper. The child, in a sense, has forgotten his purpose for heading toward his father by the time he reaches him. He has not yet developed the ability to hold in his mind his purpose for doing something. Furthermore, he is unable to remove an obstacle without forgetting where he is going.

By the eighteenth month (stage six), however, the sensory-motor child searches for objects hidden in his presence. If you dangle keys before him and place them under a pillow, and then under another and another, he will follow the pattern you used to hide them and go to the last pillow first to determine their location. He is now capable of retrieving and retracing a series of actions. The young child usually gurgles and laughs while doing this and enjoys the fun of his newly developed mental abilities.

Object permanence is a significant advancement because permanent objects are those worth knowing. The child no longer just reacts to their presence but begins to understand their properties. Object permanence, Piaget believes, is basic to the development of concepts of identity. In this first step, the child realizes the object maintains its identity even when out of sight. Later in the child's development, he will come to realize that several actions may be imposed upon an object without its basic identity being altered. For example, the child may fold aluminum foil into many shapes but still realize it is foil. The folding does not alter its identity. Obviously, the development of conceptualizations of identity is fundamental to the achievement of the various forms of conservation which begin to appear late in the preoperational stage.

Child Learns to Distinguish

By the end of the sensory-motor period, the child has had millions of perceptions helping him to sharpen his ability to distinguish among objects. All men, for example, are no longer father. The infant has miraculously assimilated and accommodated the subtle differences existing between his father and other men. In most cases, because of greater exposure, the infant can distinguish his mother at a much earlier period. At the end of this period, the infant can distinguish among certain animals. He may even have names for many of them. Consequently, he now can call to mind people, animals, objects, and some activities. For example, he may go to the door and wave bye-bye to his father going to work. There is considerable evidence that the child has stored information in his mind. When he sees a new dog and says "dog, dog," what the child is demonstrating is that he has a concept in his mind containing the structural and functional characteristics of a dog. The infant has perceived a dog, searched its mind for what fits these perceptions, and recognized that the object is a dog. What a far distance the child has come from the newborn infant who differentiates little from the environment!

Play

At the end of the sensory-motor period, children demonstrate they are capable of simple play. They may act out a role or experiment with symbolic play as in language. For example, they may say "bird, bird." This type of language play further indicates that they are capable of evoking absent objects or events. They can also store certain sensations that can be called upon at will. In other words, they are forming the rudiments of representational thought which will manifest itself more clearly in the preoperational stage. Representational thought occurs when an individual represents in his mind something not present. This may be done through symbolic play or mental images. However, this type of thought characterizes more clearly children beyond the sensory-motor period because they are less limited to external stimuli. Even so, children early in the sensory-motor period demonstrate that they are developing representational thought. For example, Piaget notes that his daughter Jacqueline, one year, four months, and three days, had a small visitor of one year, six months visit her who threw a tantrum. Jacqueline watched with interest, not having seen such activities before. The next day she screamed and stamped her feet in a similar manner. Jacqueline evoked the situation she had seen the previous day and closely duplicated it.[1]

Summary

Truly, the sensory-motor child spans a tremendous cognitive distance in two years. He grows from a reflex dominated creature to a dynamic, reacting, and sometimes exasperating rascal. He has adapted and learned how to obtain satisfaction, thereby demonstrating to some degree intelligent behavior. The child has advanced from being able to make slight discriminations to identifying objects and people. The sensory-motor child has slowly evolved to some understanding of causality by knowing objects can be removed and replaced. Object permanence has been attained. He has moved from a gurgling infant to one using verbal means of communicating. The sensory-motor child has left the early slumber of the crib to become involved and experiment in play by acting out roles and playing with language. Because he has developed these and other mental abilities, the infant is capable of moving intellectually into the next higher cognitive level of activity, the preoperational stage. There, he will begin to demonstrate the use of language beyond the level of just calling out the names of objects and continue to expand his mentality.

Cognitive Achievements

Listed below is a summary of the major cognitive achievements the child manifests by the end of the sensory-motor period.

1. Is active and develops rudiments of thinking through action.
2. Learns to perceive and identify objects.

---

[1] Jean Piaget, *Play, Dream, and Imitation,* trans. C. Gattegno and F. M. Hodgson (New York: Norton, 1951), p. 63.

3. Develops object permanence and recognizes himself as an object.
4. Realizes objects do not change in shape from different vantage points even though perception would indicate they do.
5. Late in the period, distinguishes among parents and animals.
6. Knows the names of objects.
7. Begins to have representational thought.
8. Has no language—preverbal.
9. Has rudimentary sense of direction.
10. Has developed schemes to manipulate objects, etc.
11. Searches for vanished objects.
12. Performs simple experiments on things to learn some of their properties.
13. Demonstrates means-end activity, e.g., to get objects.
14. Knows only immediate space.
15. Aware of present time. By the end of the period is aware of sequence of events and duration.

The Preoperational Period: 2-7 Years   4

The Intuitive Stage

The second stage of mental development, spanning years two through seven, is called *preoperational*. It is preoperational because the child is *not* yet capable of carrying on in her mind any *logical operations,* such as:

> ADDING: Combining
> SUBTRACTING: Taking away
> MULTIPLYING: Repeating
> DIVIDING: Repeating Subtraction
> CORRESPONDING: Aligning one row with another
> PLACING IN ORDER: This is greater than or this is less
>   than; done by comparing size, weight, age, color, etc.
> SUBSTITUTING: Replacing something similar with
>   another entity
> REVERSIBILITY: Subclasses belong to a class ⇆ a class
>   has subclasses

The preoperational child not only is unable to perform these operations, but she also cannot do certain infralogical operations. Infralogical operations are considered by Piaget to differ from logical ones in that their content is basically continuous and they have to do with physical space and time associations. The infralogical operations include such things as:

> OBSERVATION: Looking at something critically
> MEASUREMENT: How long, high, what volume, using
>   a standard homemade unit

QUANTITY: How much

TIME: Now, future, past

SERIATION: Putting objects in series by following a
pattern or constructing a hierarchy

CLASSIFICATION: Grouping according to similarities,
partitioning a group into subgroups based on some
property and arranging these in an hierarchy

SPACE: Room, home, community, country, continent,
world, universe

INTERPERSONAL REACTIONS: Getting along with
others, noting the effects of one's behavior on others

COUNTING OF OBJECTS: Realizing the meaning of
cardinal numbers (1,2,3), setting up one-to-one
correspondence

VALUES: Establishing values

Most of these logical and infralogical operations are not demonstrated by children until after the age of seven when they reach the concrete-operational level of mental development. However, the preoperational stage is very important because it serves as the foundation for all later mental growth.

Representational Thought Increases

In the preoperational period, actions become symbolically internalized in the mind. This means a child can think of moving an object before she moves it. For example, a young child wants to pull a small wagon through a doorway. She pulls the wagon almost up to the door, then stops, looks at the door, and *decides* that she needs to push the wagon back a ways before opening the door (she uses her mind in visualizing, at least to some degree, what will happen if she opens the door now). The child does this, lays down the wagon handle, goes to the door, opens it wide, and then goes to the wagon and pulls it through the door. By so doing, she is demonstrating that her mind is capable of representing actions (e.g., opening the door) and that she must have the capability of storing such actions in some form to be called upon as she demands. The sensory-motor child may perform the same above act if she sees her sister or brother pull the wagon, that is, she will *imitate* their actions. The preoperational child is capable of imitating these actions in the absence of a model, further demonstrating her representional ability. She also has the ability to combine several actions to produce a new idea in her mind and to think of one action and then annul it by another in her mind.

Piaget believes the performing of these internal (cognitive) actions is fundamental to the development of more complex operational abilities. In other words, the path to logical development progresses as follows:

EXTERNAL ACTIONS	COGNITIVE INTERNAL	CONCRETE
Sensory-Motor Activity $\longrightarrow$	ACTIONS $\longrightarrow$	OPERATIONS
Ages 0–2—Imitative Behavior	Ages 2–7—In Absence of a Model	Ages 7–11

Language Accelerates Thought

Because she is internalizing actions during the preoperational period, the child uses more symbols, such as words, to represent actions and objects. By the time she reaches this period, she has already learned to use words and construct some simple sentences, e.g., "Mother goes out, Daddy comes." However, the sensory-motor child is unable to differentiate between the object a word stands for and that object's function. She uses the word *Mommy*, not meaning mother but a host of satisfactions that occur from mother. She sees her father carrying a briefcase into the study and confuses the briefcase for the action, father is leaving. She does not understand the briefcase is used for carrying things and that only sometimes it indicates father is leaving. A sweater on her mother may indicate to the sensory-motor child that she "goes away." Comparatively speaking, the preoperational child appears more rational. Her mother may put on a sweater, and she realizes it is an object to keep her mother warm. The wearing of it does not necessarily mean the event, mother is going away. The preoperational child often labels or names objects. This does not indicate, however, that she has a logical system, for she may call an object long one time and short the next, depending on whether the length or width impresses her.

Piaget believes the advent of language accelerates the development of thought. This is so because language makes possible verbal exchanges, internalizations of actions, and words. It allows for social changes which eventually contribute to the child's becoming less egocentric in her view of the environment. As a result, she soon learns that there are perceptions and views differing from her own. The development of language makes it possible for children to think of a series of actions not present and to perform these more rapidly than would be the case were they to act them out physically, as they did in the sensory-motor stage. Language, as a consequence, contributes to the speed of thought and allows for a wider range of possibilities. Because this is so, a child may use her thought to think beyond the immediate and move into the future. As a result, time begins to assume a broader perspective.

Through language the child frees herself from the limitation of acting on objects, which characterized her sensory-motor behavior. By the middle of the preoperational stage, most children have mastered the basic form of their language, enabling their thought to progress at an even more rapid rate.

No Transformations

The preoperational child's thinking tends to be more static than mobile. For example, if you draw a series of pictures on cards showing how a pencil falls so that there is only one diagram per card and then ask the child to place the cards in order showing how they fall, you will find the child has difficulty doing this. She may correctly choose the first pencil and the last one in the series but mix up all the rest.

A child of this age apparently *focuses* her attention on individual cards or states without the ability to picture in her mind a sequence of events. In other words, she cannot grasp a series of *transformations*. This can be further demonstrated by having children watch a glass of water being filled. Ask them to diagram in steps how it is filled. Most preoperational children experience difficulty in preparing these diagrams.

No Reverse Thinking

A preoperational child also cannot perform reversible thought. Asked what a duck is, she will say it is a bird. If then asked if there would be any ducks if all birds were killed, she would probably say yes. To an adult this thinking is clearly inconsistent, but the child is unable to see this because she does not yet have a rational mind.

An adult might try to force the child to be consistent by repeating or asking additional questions. Confronted with such demands, the child will probably respond by giving irrational answers, such as, "Ducks go swimming or fly away." She gives these answers because she is not yet capable of performing reverse-thinking operations, and, even if given instructions in what the answer should be, she will not retain or understand them. She is not yet capable of reversing her thoughts and cannot understand the logic illustrated below.

Ducks (a subclass) belong to (the class) birds.

If birds (the class) are destroyed, then the (subclass) ducks are also destroyed.

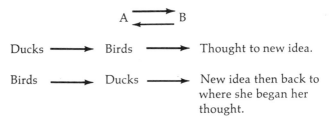

Mathematically, this is the same as saying that the child should be able to do the following:

$$1 + 2 = 3$$
$$3 - 2 = 1$$

This is much above the ability of a child of this stage because she is incapable of performing the reversible thought sequences or the mental operations required in *adding* or *subtracting*. Furthermore, the preoperational child cannot reason about her thinking. She is still incapable of analyzing, synthesizing, and evaluating thoughts.

Fantasy and Realism

A child of this age also has difficulty distinguishing truth from fantasy. For example, all that she sees on television may be true to her. This is so because she cannot comprehend *realism*. She perceives everything as having the same reality, and the way she sees things is the way they are.

Because of these mental inabilities of the preoperational child, parents may mistake their child's stretching the truth as fabricating when, in fact, it is due to a lack of cognitive development. A parent may want to correct such poor thinking by explaining, for example, how a lake was actually formed.

Piaget tells the story of how he attempted to do this with his young son. One day, as he was walking with him in Switzerland, they passed a lake. He asked his son, "How was the lake formed?" His son replied, "A giant threw a rock and made it." Piaget replied that this was not so and described how the lake had been formed by a glacier. He then asked him to repeat his explanation to insure the boy understood, and it appeared that the child did.

Several months later, Piaget and his son again passed the same lake, and Piaget asked him how it was formed. The boy replied, "A giant threw a rock and made it." This artificialistic explanation was maintained in spite of the previous efforts of the father. The child was not cognitively ready at his age to incorporate a nonartificial explanation for the formation of the lake into his mind. Furthermore, he believed that the way he perceived how the lake was formed was the same for everybody.

Animistic and Artificialistic Explanations

The preoperational child is artificialistic and animistic in her view of the world. She is *artificialistic* because she considers all objects and events as being made by humans. The child thinks the sun, moon, mountains, lakes, etc., were made by people. She is animistic because she endows phenomena and objects, such as wind, rocks, buttons, dishes, etc., with psychological and logical attributes. For example, in her descriptions of motion, she might say, "Roller skates roll and rocks fall because they want to or are mean because they hurt my toe." Of course, roller skates and rocks are not capable of having the human qualities of wanting or meanness. The child may also attribute human characteristics to plants and animals. "Plants lose their leaves in the fall because they wish to change how they look." "Wolves don't like people." "Smokey the Bear likes people." Plants cannot wish, and wolves and bears are not able to mentally think of what they like and dislike.

False (Pseudo) Learning

The above episode about Piaget and his son not only illustrates artificial thinking and problems with reality, but also that parents and teachers can be fooled about what a child is learning. In the lake episode, Piaget believed his son had learned the scientific explanation of its origin. The child did initially give his father satisfaction by retelling him what he had said about the lake's history. Unfortunately, this scientific explanation was not accommodated into the mind of the child. Piaget would say that the child's parroting his explanation without a real change of mental awareness (accommodation) was an example of false (pseudo) learning.

Misconceptions Are Corrected

Parents and teachers should not be concerned about artificialistic explanations. They are natural. As preoperational children experience life, their minds increasingly progress in development, and they naturally correct these misconceptions. By the end of the concrete-operational stage, most of these explanations will have been replaced by more adult ones, without the cost of pseudo-learning.

Then too, fantasy probably is a necessary ingredient in maintaining a child's ego. For it is through fantasy that children can win. Since they do not yet have sufficient mentality to argue and win with adults or really interact well with the environment, they use fantasy to cope with what confronts them.

Since a child's fantasies appear real to her, it is often better to accept this fact and interact with the child accordingly. For example, if the child is afraid to go to sleep in the dark because of the "boogie man," the parent might accept this and say, "Did you know the boogie man is afraid of teddy bears? If you have your teddy bear, the boogie man won't come in your room." By such a response, the parent will lessen the anxiety of the child. To try to argue that there are no boogie men probably would be futile.

Social, Physical and Logical-Mathematical Experience

Piaget looks upon knowledge as being derived from *social, physical* and *logical-mathematical* experience. In *physical experience,* for example, a child might be given a ruler and told the name of the stick is a ruler. The child learns the name with little difficulty. She may imprint or store it in her mind in some representational way. However, in learning how to use the ruler effectively, the child has to reason—use logic and mathematical thinking. In other words, she has *logical-mathematical* experience. If she does not use her mind in this manner so that she actually thinks out, reasons, and concludes how to use the ruler, the child will not retain what is taught and pseudo-learning will be the result. In *social experience*, a child may learn how to better interact with people and note different views or perceptions of phenomena. Piaget believes you cannot teach a child to use her mind. All a teacher or parent can do is set up the environment to *facilitate* its use. The child must do the thinking herself, and, when she does, real as opposed to pseudo-learning occurs.

Social Interaction Lessens Egocentrism

As already indicated by the discussions on realism, animism, and artificialism, the preoperational child is highly egocentric. She assumes the way she sees phenomena is the way all people see them. The preoperational child is not aware of the possibility of conflicting views relative to the solution of a problem. When the child talks, particularly in the early part of this period, she often carries on a monologue, oblivious to another person. It is as though the child believes it is sufficient to just say something to be understood. The idea that communication involves insuring that the listener understands is not realized. As a consequence, the child is often surprised that she does not communicate.

Piaget believes that social interaction plays a major role in lessening this type of egocentricity.

Play

Because of their egocentricity, preoperational children are incapable of playing any cooperative types of games with other children. They may appear to be playing a game, but what really is happening is that each child is playing a game independently of the others, with little or no concern about the actions of the others. This process of two or more children playing games independently is called *parallel game playing*, and it may persist far beyond the preoperational level in diminishing degrees. The preoperational child also has difficulty in playing games because she does not realize play and reality may operate under different rules. This misconception occurs because her beliefs have not been derived from logical operations but are arbitrary. The child has beliefs but does not know how or why. Furthermore, children before age four will not even follow any rules. They do not realize that it is by mutual agreement that rules are determined.

Preoperational children often become fascinated with "make believe" play. They like to play house, store, etc. They will spend long periods of time playing with blocks and building things with playing cards or certain types of construction toys. The things they build represent trains, cars, houses, castles, forts, etc. Piaget believes this play fascination, in part, manifests itself because these children are now capable of more representational thought. He further thinks that this type of representation is transferred to word symbols.

Reasoning Processes

Two basic reasoning processes used by adults are inductive and deductive thinking. These processes are characterized as follows:

Inductive Thinking—Reasoning from the specific to the general.

Deductive Thinking—Reasoning from the general to the specific.

Example of Inductive Thinking:

A. This apple has a stem.   Specific Apple

B. Another apple has a stem.

    therefore

C. All apples have stems.   General Conclusion

Example of Deductive Thinking:

A. All apples have stems.   Generalization

B. This is an apple.

    therefore

C. It has a stem.   Specific Conclusion

Often individuals confuse these two processes. This confusion can be eliminated by remembering deductive thinking requires something to be deduced. *Deduce* comes from the Latin *deducere* meaning to lead or draw down. Essentially, what a person is doing in deductive reasoning is thinking away from or down from a generalization. By knowing the nature of deductive thinking, it is easy to recall that inductive thinking proceeds in the opposite direction from specific to general. These types of thinking characterize rational processes found in more advanced stages of cognitive development, e.g., ascending and descending a classification hierarchy, as will be pointed out later in the text.

Preoperational children are incapable of reasoning inductively or deductively. They can, however, reason *transductively*. This means they think usually *from particular to particular*. For example, a parent may prepare pancake batter and then heat the frying pan. To the child, preparing pancakes means the pan shall be heated. If she comes into the kitchen another day and sees the frying pan being heated, she may think that pancakes are being prepared. Her thought really is not based on logical processes, but contiguity of phenomena she sees. She believes if some *things occur together, there is a causal relationship*. Another example of transductive reasoning is:

Santa Claus comes down a chimney.

Our house has no chimney.

No chimney → No Santa Claus

The child concludes that Santa Claus will not come because she juxtaposes Santa Clause and chimneys in her mind and believes that a chimney is required for Santa Claus to visit a home. The child, in this case, centers on one element of Santa's visit, his coming down the chimney, and, as a result, draws a faulty conclusion. She does not reason that Santa Claus could come in the door or window.

Sometimes, the child using transductive reasoning does come up with a correct answer. However, Piaget cautions that this does not indicate the mental path the child followed was anything other than transductive. The preoperational child as yet has not developed the idea of logical necessity or physical causality, but still relates things mainly because of juxtaposition.

Piaget believes that transductive reasoning occurs before and serves as a basis for the more sophisticated thinking processes following in the later stages of mental development. Because of this preliminary reasoning ability, preoperational children seldom use such connectives as, *because, therefore,* and *although,* in their language.

Semilogic Develops

Semilogic, however, begins to appear. This means the child uses a logical pattern of thinking, but only in one direction. For example, place four colored counters—red, white, blue, and green—next to corresponding colors of dolls, as shown in the diagram. Pick up the colored counters and place them in a toy truck going from counter to counter in order, but leaving the dolls in place. Ask a child why the blue counter was picked up third, etc. The child probably will say because the truck stopped at the blue doll third. She can map in her mind

FORWARD-DIRECTION THINKING

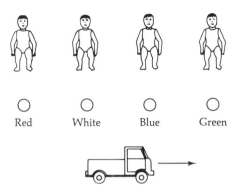

| Red | White | Blue | Green |

that the blue counter goes with the blue doll. But, if you ask four year olds the itinerary the truck took, even though they can see the counters in the truck and the dolls on the table, they cannot retrace in their minds the sequence. Their mental semilogic is limited to forward-direction thinking only.[1]

Conservation

Preoperational children have not yet developed an understanding of the conservation of number, matter, volume, or weight. That is, they cannot understand that changing an object physically by length, shape, direction, or position does not alter the sum of its material.

CONSERVATION OF WEIGHT

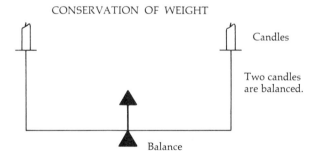

Candles

Two candles are balanced.

Balance

Then one candle is broken into two pieces.

A preoperational child is presented with the information in the diagram above and asked, What do you think will happen if the broken candle is placed back on the balance? The child will probably say the broken candle will weigh

[1] Myron Rosskopf, Leslie Steele, and Stanley Taback, eds., *Cognitive Development Research and Mathematical Education*, proceedings of a conference conducted at Columbia University, October 1970 (Washington, D.C.: NCTM, 1971), pp. 4–5.

more than the unbroken one even though she knows that the two pieces comprise one candle and the candles were in balance before one of them was broken. This faulty thinking occurs because the child has not accommodated the realization that changing the form of something does not alter the amount of matter present. The child is fooled by her perceptions. She thinks that in the rolled clay there is more because it looks bigger, instead of reasoning that nothing has been added or taken away. The preoperational child is said, therefore, to be *perception bound.* However, during the latter part of the preoperational period, the child will learn *object constancy*—objects are the same even though they may be placed in different surroundings. This realization is basic to developing conservation of number, weight, and volume in the concrete stage. The comprehension of conservational principles will be discussed in greater detail in the next chapter.

Number, Quantity, Measurement, and Velocity

Children of this age do not understand the significance of number, quantity, measurement, or velocity. They may know how to count but not comprehend the meaning of *number.* For example, you may ask a six-year-old boy if he can count. The child may reply yes. If you place your fingers in front of him and have him count, he will probably count up to ten. This counting, however, does not indicate the child knows what he is doing; he is merely demonstrating a memorized series of names, without knowing their significance.

Before children can comprehend the meaning of number, they must first develop in their minds certain operations. They have to know the names of the numbers, place *objects in a series, and order them.* In ordering, they must realize that each of the members of a series is ordered according to some characteristic and that they are not equal. They must also be able to *cardinate*—ask the question, How many?

Since the preoperational child cannot *conserve number,* if you place five straws close to each other in front of her and then spread them out, she thinks there are more. She does not realize that rearranging objects does not affect the number present. Because the preoperational child cannot comprehend infralogical and logical operations, she also cannot yet perform measurement and velocity tasks.

Time and Space

The preoperational child's concept of time has broadened since the sensory-motor stage. She now thinks not only of the present but the past and future as well. Her extension of time, however, is limited to short periods not distant from the present, and her ability to predict time and arrive somewhere on time is very limited.

The child's concept of space has broadened from the area in which she acts to the house, yard, and the neighborhood. However, the understanding of state, country, and world are still undeveloped.

Perception

Children in this period have problems replicating what they see. Piaget has discovered that this is partially due to the fact they do not yet have good structuring processes in their minds to accommodate what they perceive. For example, before age four, all closed figures, e.g., rectangles, circles, triangles, and ellipses, are copied as curved, closed lines.

To a four year old, rectangles and triangles have curved corners.

When a child develops in her mind the structure of a square, she no longer has difficulty drawing it properly. Further evidence of the role mental structure plays is demonstrated during the ages of six and seven. These children tend to draw what they know, have in their minds, rather than what they perceive. They draw the two eyes and the four wheels in the manner shown in the diagram because they know in their minds that these are part of the objects they are seeing.

Preoperational children draw what they know
rather than what they perceive.

 Two eyes in profile

 Four wheels on one
side of a pick-up truck

Children of these ages also have trouble drawing in the proper perspective. No matter how they see an object, they will often tend to draw it from the side

No matter what their perception,
they draw from a side view.

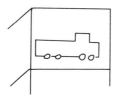

Table is drawn from above,
but truck is drawn from one side.

view. For example, if they see a truck on top of a table and look down at it as if from an airplane, they draw it from the side rather than from the top. Piaget says that what children do not *mentally understand they tend to deform.*

Summary

As indicated in this chapter, preoperational children widen their perceptions of the environment and demonstrate the gradual evolution of structures providing the base for operational thinking that unfolds in the next stage of cognitive development. Representational thought has increased, contributing to the acceleration of language development. They now speak using fairly complex sentence structures but still seldom use connectives in their language. Although preoperational children are still relatively egocentric, they are losing this egocentricity, as indicated by their ability to play games and follow rules. They still, however, have difficulty differentiating among truth, fantasy and realism. Semilogic, using logical patterns of thinking but only in one direction, and transductive thinking have evolved. Toward the end of the period these children begin their hierarchical path toward developing the various types of conservation, starting with conserving substance. Their conceptualizations of space and time have broadened considerably from those of the sensory-motor period.

Cognitive Achievement

Listed below is a summary of the major cognitive achievements the child manifests by the end of the preoperational period.

1. Cannot do operational thinking, particularly reversible thinking.
2. Is perception bound—mainly acts on perceptive impulse.
3. Is egocentric—the way he sees it is the way it is. Social interaction reduces this.
4. Does not follow rules in games up to age four. Language develops but egocentric —early part of the stage may carry on monologue. Seldom uses connectives— *because, therefore, although.*
5. Can count but does not know numbers.
6. Is static thinker—fails to make transformations, does not think through a series of operations, but situation to situation.
7. Develops semilogic, but in one direction only.
8. Cannot distinguish between fantasy and reality.
9. Is animistic—gives inanimate objects living attributes.
10. Is artificialistic—believes humans have created mountains, lakes, moon, sun. Gives magical and omnipotent explanations for physical phenomena.
11. Exhibits pseudo-learning.
12. Aware of present, future, and past, but of short durations.
13. Broadens concept of space to include house, yard, neighborhood.
14. Can not solve conservation problems with possible exception of conservation of matter late in the period.

15. Draws geometrical figures, such as the square and triangle, as having curved corners or points.
16. Draws what knows rather than what sees.

> **Go to MEDIAPAK B, "The Sensory-Motor and Preoperational Periods." When you have completed it, return to this text and take the following self-evaluation inventory for the first part of the MEDIAPAK and Chapter 3. Your knowledge of the second part of the MEDIAPAK and Chapter 4 will be reinforced by administering Piagetian interviews.**

Self-evaluation Inventory

Sensory-Motor Period

Directions: Listed below are some of the main topics covered in Chapter 3 and MEDIAPAK B. Read each statement and rate it on the scale TWICE: once according to what you knew about the topic before starting this part of the program and again according to what you have learned after completing it. Circle the appropriate number and mark B for before and A for after next to the number as indicated below.

	Student Evaluation		
Topic	*Low*	*Moderate*	*High*
Example: Important Piagetian mental operations.	①B 2	3 4	5 ⑥A
1. The role of action in influencing cognition.	1 2	3 4	5 6
2. The reason for calling this stage sensory-motor.	1 2	3 4	5 6
3. How grasping contributes to cognition.	1 2	3 4	5 6
4. The six stages of the sensory-motor period.	1 2	3 4	5 6
5. The stages toward object permanence.	1 2	3 4	5 6
6. The child's progression toward distinguishing ability.	1 2	3 4	5 6
7. The development of play and understanding of rules.	1 2	3 4	5 6
8. The development of concepts of time and space.	1 2	3 4	5 6
9. The development of naming ability.	1 2	3 4	5 6

Now that you have assessed your growth after completing this part of the program, review those areas where you indicate there is either a lack of growth or confidence about the topic.

To reinforce your knowledge of Chapter 4 and
MEDIAPAK B, turn to Chapter 10 and read how to
administer Piagetian interviews. Then select eight
to ten preoperational activities from those listed
in Chapter 11. Interview at least two preoperational-
aged children using these activities. Record your
results on a form similar to the one included in
Chapter 10.

The Concrete-
Operational Period:
7-11 Years 5

The concrete-operational period begins for most children around age seven and terminates, according to Piaget, at age eleven. It is called *concrete* because children's thought is restricted to what they encounter in direct experience. They think about objects that do exist and their properties, for example, weight, color, and texture, and they think about the actions they can do with these objects. Moreover, during these years, children slowly develop many mental operations such as:

1. Classifying in various ways, grouping things into a class or subclass.
2. Doing one-to-one correspondence.
3. Reversing thought processes A$\rightarrow$ B and A $\leftarrow$B.
4. Performing many mathematical operations: adding, subtracting, substituting, multiplying, dividing, ordering elements or events in time.

As the concrete-operational child interacts with the environment, he increasingly calls upon his experiences and his developing operational abilities for direction. The development of operational behavior enables the individual to make great mental advancements. Piaget believes this is so because operational ability is the keystone of intelligence. He says, "Intelligence is born of action. Any act of intelligence—whether it be on the part of a man involved in scientific research, or the child of seven and eight, consists of operations, carrying out operations, and coordinating them among themselves."[1]

Less Stimulus Bound

The concrete-operational child is not as easily fooled by perceptual differences as is his preoperational counterpart. For example, a six-year-old preoperational child, shown a wide, shallow glass with a few ounces of colored water that is then

---

[1] Jean Piaget, *Saturday Review*, May 20, 1967, p. 38.

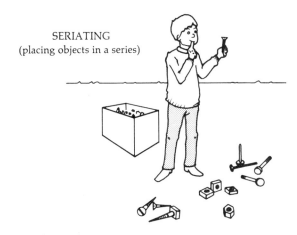

SERIATING
(placing objects in a series)

poured into a tall, narrow glass, thinks the tall glass has more liquid in it than the wide one. The six year old makes this mistake because his judgment is determined mainly by perception. A concrete-operational child, however, will say the amount in either glass is the same because he *reasons* that nothing has been added or taken away from the containers. This child is, therefore, less *stimulus bound*, but his thinking is stimulus related because he still relies heavily on perceptions instead of abstract reasoning in coming to conclusions.

Conservation

Conservation is the realization that changing an object physically, for example, the shape, length, direction, and position, does not alter the amount present.

The concrete-operational child conserves or realizes that altering the shape of material does not modify the amount present. This use of the mind to determine the reasonableness of something rather than relying on perception fundamentally demarks the concrete individual from one in the next cognitively lower stage. Because this is so, concrete children, when presented with a problem, are more likely to think about it before answering. Their answers and explanations also appear more rational. In this stage, for example, children begin counting mentally rather than counting on their fingers.

Piaget believes a major achievement of the concrete stage is the continued and constructive refining of concepts plus the discovery of how concepts are interrelated. For example, children, through their interaction with materials in the environment, gradually begin to evolve a conceptual understanding of conservation. First they develop conservation of substance. For example, they understand that, if a ball of putty is rolled into a hot dog shape, it has no more putty than before, unlike the preoperational child, who thinks the longer shape has more mass. Although it is reasonable to expect a child conserving substance to generalize this to conserving length, weight, or volume, such is not the case. Refer to the chart below for the types of conservation and the approximate age level of attainment.

Types of Conservation	Age
Conservation of Substance: realizes amount of substance does not change by dividing it	6–7
Conservation of Number: realizes rearranging objects does not change their number	6½–7
Conservation of a Continuous Quantity: realizes pouring liquid from one container to another does not change the quantity	6–7
Conservation of Length: realizes, e.g., unbending a semicircle-shaped wire does not change its length	7–8
Conservation of Area: realizes the area covered by a paper cut in half is just as much as if it were whole	7–8
Conservation of Weight: realizes a mashed piece of clay weighs the same as when it was a sphere	9–12
Conservation of Displacement Volume: realizes that two halves of a ball immersed in liquid will occupy as much volume as if they were a whole sphere	11–12 and beyond

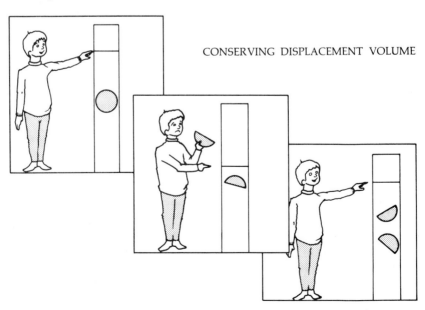

CONSERVING DISPLACEMENT VOLUME

There is evidence, however, that a large number of students junior and senior high school age still have difficulty understanding conservation. Replicating some of Piaget's work, Elkind found, in testing 469 students in junior and senior high school, that 87 percent achieved conservation of substance and 47 percent achieved conservation of volume.[2] He further found significant differences between boys and girls in the attainment of conservation. This he attributes largely to the expected role of the male in our society; for example, boys are expected to be more analytical than girls. His research also indicates that the longer students remain in school, the better they become at conserving. Presumably, this is due to their having experiences requiring conservation, particularly in science classes.

Consequently, the mental, connective process of interrelating perceptual experiences with conservation evolves relatively slowly. The child first demonstrates no conserving, then conserves in some ways but not others, and, finally, at age twelve or beyond relies almost totally on his mind. He becomes certain *logically*, rather than perceptually, as to whether things are *visibly* conserved or not. The child's conceptual understanding of conservation slowly evolves as his mind develops, providing he has experiences with this type of thinking.

Having opportunities to manipulate substances involving conservation undoubtedly contributes to better comprehending these principles and facilitates the learning of higher-level concepts at a later time in the development of the child.

Mathematical Operations

The concrete-operational child begins to increase his ability to perform mathematical operations. This does not mean that at the beginning of this period he immediately begins to add, subtract, or act in other ways operationally, nor does it mean that all of the types of operational thinking develop simultaneously. Operations do not occur in isolation; they are connected to other operations. By

ORDERING (small to large)

---

[2] David Elkind, "Quantity Conceptions in Junior and Senior High School Students," *Child Development* 32 (1961): 551–60.

the end of the concrete period, the child is able to perform such logical and mathematical operations as adding (+) or combining, subtracting (—) or separating, multiplying (×), dividing (÷), placing in order (>), substituting (=), and reversing (⇆). These operations usually appear first in the child's logic before they are used in mathematics. For example, the child may combine oranges and apples into a group called fruit. Later he performs the similar mathematical operation of adding one orange and one apple to form the group fruit. It is interesting to note that children develop the ability to order in one direction a year or more before they can reverse order. That is, they might be able to order things from small to large but have difficulty ordering from large to small. This partially explains why some children who can add have problems subtracting.

Number

One of the first indications that operational thought is taking place occurs when the child shows he really understands *number*. Piaget believes this comprehension manifests itself only after an individual has developed certain logical attributes. Parents and teachers often have the mistaken idea that, if a child can count, he knows the meaning of number. Preoperational children often can count "wum," "two," "tree," but "two" is only a sound that follows "wum." For a child to truly understand number, he must first be able to ask mentally how many objects are involved and classify them. For example, the child may look at his feet and say "shoes" and then ask himself *"How many do I have?"* and come up with the statement, "I have two shoes." He first classified the shoes and then determined how many there were before he finally arrived at the answer. A parent or teacher seeking to determine whether or not a child understood number in the above example, would ask, "How do you know you only have two shoes?" In other words, they would ask the child to give some *justification* for his answer. If the child gives a rational explanation, they know he really comprehends number and has not, by trial and error, just happened on the correct response.

A simple test to determine whether children ages five through seven comprehend number is to ask them to count their fingers on both hands. They usually can count fairly well. Then ask, "If the tenth finger were number one, what would be the numbers of the longest finger in each hand?" Those not conserving will have difficulty.

TEST FOR DETERMINING KNOWLEDGE OF NUMBER

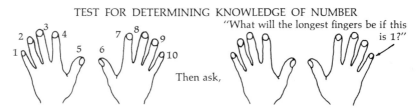

"What will the longest fingers be if this is 1?"

Then ask,

Children cannot count with understanding unless they know the meaning of numbers. In order to do this, they must realize the following:

1. All objects included in one group are treated as though they are alike and belong to the group being counted (arrive at a cardinal number). They have to disregard

object differences in classifying them in a set in order to arrive at their number, while still realizing that the objects are separate entities. For example, apples may differ in appearance, but they are still apples.

2. The children must further understand that the number of something is dependent upon its location in a series. For example, the third finger is that, if it is in third place on the hand. The tip of it can be crossed with another finger so that it becomes the second or fourth tip, and when this is done its number changes.

3. The child must count things in some sequence (order) and not jump around. He must realize that the number of objects in a group remains the same regardless of how they are arranged (conservation of number). For example, if the child truly understands conservation of number, he will not be fooled by the following exercise in the illustration below. Preoperational children usually say the second

STRAWS PLACED CLOSE TOGETHER

The straws are then moved far apart and the child is asked, "Are there more, less, or the same number of straws now?"

STRAWS MOVED APART

group of straws has more. You can even have them count the straws in both groups, but they will still think there are more widely spread straws because these children do not conserve number.

4. Furthermore, the child must mentally perform one-to-one correspondence. For instance, in the example above, he must match objects before they were spread out with those after they have been moved and realize they do not differ in number.

Counting is a rote activity involving little cognitive experience unless it is used as a basis for further rational involvement. Conceptually grasping the meaning of number and applying it to a situation requires considerable logical-mathematical development.

Classification

Being able to classify objects or ideas is basic to intellectual thought. Developing classificational skills is paramount for us to order and easily locate information in our mind. Once classes are mentally coded, we can use this information to better interact with other entities in new situations. For example, a young child soon learns the class *silverware*. He can be taken to another home, told to get some silverware from the kitchen, and do it with little difficulty. The silverware may be entirely different from those the child has seen in his own home, but he is not fooled by the differences. Once he has established the characteristics of a class in his mind, the child retains this information and interacts in more sophisticated ways as a result.

As with conservation, there are progressive stages of classificational development. The sequence of some of these stages, beginning at age three of the preoperational period and progressing through to the formal level are included here in order to give you a better comprehension of the development of classificational abilities.

Classificational Sequence	*Age*
Grouping Perceptually: sees single characteristic	3–4
Grouping Mentally: abstracts common property	3–4
Multiple Classification: classifies by more than one property	4–5
Grouping by Recognizing Differences: sees like and unlike qualities	4–5
Class Inclusion: forms subclasses and includes them in major classes	5–6
Grouping by Ascending Hierarchy	7–8
Grouping by Descending Hierarchy	9–10
Establishing Multiple Criteria: forms relatively complex classification system	11–14

Classificational Sequence

Grouping Perceptually. A lower-aged preoperational child eventually becomes able to group objects by one characteristic. However, it is important to realize that this grouping is almost entirely a perceptual activity. The child sees, for example, red blocks, and he pushes them into one group. He does not, in this first stage, originate in his mind, "There are red and white blocks. I shall separate these into groups." This occurs in the next developmental step.

Grouping Mentally. In the second stage of classificational development, the child actually abstracts. He mentally realizes that objects may be grouped by some common property such as color or size.

Multiple Classification. Late in the preoperational stage children usually realize that objects may be classified in more than one way. For example, if you give them different colored paper cut in various shapes—triangles, circles, etc.— and sizes, they realize that the papers can be grouped by color, shape, and size.

Grouping by Recognizing Differences. As children interact with objects, they slowly come to realize mentally that objects can have different characteristics, for example, different sizes, shapes, textures, and colors, while, at the same time, having a common characteristic. They learn to group objects by these common characteristics.

Class Inclusion. Around ages five or six, children may realize that a major class, cut pieces of paper, for example, may be composed of subclasses: triangles, circles, etc. These, in turn, may belong to other groups: red or white, etc. If you ask a child what all the shapes are made of, he will probably answer paper. If there are far more red paper shapes than white, and you ask, "Are there more red shapes than paper?" The child may be confused. If he has not yet developed to the class inclusion stage, he will be overcome by the *perceptual impact of the red* and will say there are more red shapes than paper. The late preoperational child in transition from this stage to the concrete-operational will say, on the other hand, "No, there is more paper than red shapes." He realizes that the red papers (the subgroup) belong to the major category *paper.*

Grouping by Ascending Hierarchy. In the concrete-operational period, children can construct ascending hierarchies. At the ages of seven and eight, most children are aware of subgroups and major groups and can group these subgroups into the major class.

Grouping by Descending Hierarchy. Although a child can group things into an ascending hierarchy, he cannot necessarily put them into a descending one. The ability to do this does not manifest itself until around nine or ten. To perform this classification task the child must be able to reverse his thinking operations. Some children, however, who may demonstrate *reversibility* still cannot descend a hierarchy. They have not generalized the reversible operation fully, as yet.

Establishing Multiple Criteria. Not until the next stage, formal-operational, do children complete the classificational sequence. During that stage, they will be able to construct multiple criteria for establishing a relatively complex classificational system, similar to those used in locating objects in a storehouse.

A main outcome of the concrete stage, therefore, is that the child constructs class and relation concepts with which he can more effectively order encounters in the environment. He conceptually organizes his environment into cognitive structures—ideas. Each new encounter does not require extensive examination but can be classified according to structure and function and checked with classificational schemes in his mind. This allows for much more efficient responses.

Limited Hypotheses

The concrete child further demonstrates his mental progress by making limited hypotheses. He can think what will happen if something is added to the volume of a container, both to the one receiving the liquid and the one being depleted. However, he is usually limited to making only one hypothesis, typically involving only one variable. A child is better able to do this if he sees the containers because he still has difficulty mentally visualizing a problem and acting upon it to come to an answer. This mental holding ability while performing operations does not occur to a great degree usually until a child is well into the formal-operational stage.

Understanding of Space and Time

The concrete-operational child's conceptual understanding of space and time has broadened to include some notions of geographical space and historical time. He can think of the area of his city and state and has some notions of different cities and places. These children become fascinated with historical episodes and their place in time, for example, pilgrims, pioneers, Indians, and astronauts.

Action Representation

All of the advancements of the concrete child are due to his increasing tendency to use his mind to represent physical action. Mental action takes the place of physical action. For example, using the example mentioned before, the concrete-operational child knows that, when water is poured from a wide, flat jar to a slender one, the amount of liquid has not changed. He will probably explain: "If you return the water to the wide jar, you will have the same volume as before." He mentally performs the action of refilling the wide jar with water, thus exhibiting reversibility. In this period, then, semilogic, thinking in only one direction, turns into logic. The child thinks about objects, their properties, and the possible actions that can be performed on them. Using the mind to perform such operations characterizes children in this period and provides the foundation for more sophisticated patterns of thought in the next stage of development.

Cognitive Achievements

Listed below is a summary of the major cognitive achievements the child manifests by the end of the concrete-operational period. Review it and picture how an individual behaves when he demonstrates each of these characteristics. By acting on the information in this way, you should better comprehend and retain the characteristics of the concrete-operational stage.

1. Becomes logical and does reversible thinking.
2. Mainly reasons about things, but has difficulty with verbal propositions.
3. Analyzes.
4. Measures.
5. Is aware of variables.
6. Understands part and whole relationships.
7. Understands and uses logic of classes. Demonstrates class inclusion, ascending and descending hierarchies. ·
8. Conserves number, mass, weight, and sometimes volume.

9. Accepts the ethics and rules of authorities, parents, etc.
10. Performs the following mental *operations:*
    a. Combining
    b. Separating
    c. Ordering
    d. Seriating
    e. Multiplying or repeating
    f. Dividing
    g. Substituting
    h. Doing one-to-one correspondence
11. Still has difficulty with complex verbal problems.

> **Go to MEDIAPAK C, "The Concrete-Operational Period." When you have completed it, return to this text and select ten concrete-operational activities from Chapter 12. Use these to interview at least two concrete-operational–aged children. Record your results on an interview form similar to the one in Chapter 10. You might also like to administer the "Concrete-Operational Reasoning Test" found in Appendix A. Then continue with Chapter 6.**

The Formal-
Operational Period:
11-14 Years 6

Characteristics of This Stage

During adolescence an individual's physiology undergoes an upheaval. The child's body slowly develops into the more mature male or female. Similarly, the cognitive ability of the adolescent accelerates its evolution toward maturity.

Piaget calls this stage *formal-operational* because the type of reasoning manifested is systematic and involves logically complex processes. Operations no longer are restricted to use solely on concrete objects but can be performed on other operations as well. As a result of this development, the formal individual can now solve all types of problems that can be resolved only through the use of higher levels of logical operations such as:

1. Hypothetical-deductive reasoning
2. Reflexive thinking
3. Reasoning with proportions and ratios
4. Control of variables in an experiment
5. Syllogistic reasoning
6. Probability
7. Combinatorial logic
8. Abstract reasoning
9. Comprehension of allegory
10. Propositional thinking
11. Acceptance of contrary-to-fact assumptions
12. Performance of second-order operations (Thinking about thought itself)
13. Formulation of theories
14. Conceiving of idealistic societies

Performing higher levels of reasoning and abstract thought requires individuals to follow logical patterns and rules. Formal-operational children use their minds to a higher degree than those in the stages below them to check what is perceived. They are not overcome by perceptions such as optical illusions as easily as individuals in the earlier stages. Because higher levels of thinking are structured and require that definite operational patterns and processes be followed, they are more formal in structure. Think for a moment of higher mathematics such as algebra and calculus or of the writings of St. Thomas Aquinas and Plato and you will grasp the meaning of formalistic reasoning.

Formal-operational individuals differ considerably from those in the concrete-operational stage. They no longer are limited to solving concrete types of problems but can think in terms of abstractions and multiple hypotheses. They understand and resolve relatively complex verbal problems and perform complex logic. They symbolically represent thought processes and act or reflect on them, e.g., A may be greater, less, or the same as B, and it may be related in similar ways to C. Therefore, C is related to A in the following ways. . . . They may also stipulate what additional information is required to definitely know the relationship of A to B and C. Another example of formal thinking is solving ratio problems such as $A/B = X/Y$. The quantities for A, B, and Y may be given, and the student is to solve for X. In other words, the formal mind often functions in an algebraic manner, letting symbols represent ideas and categories while simultaneously performing mental operations on them. Furthermore, the formal mind utilizes several operations to resolve problems and to apply hypotheses to their solutions.

More Externally Stimulus Free

Consequently, the formal-operational individual's thinking is more likely to be internally rather than externally stimulated. That is, an external stimulus is not necessary to set off thinking. The formal individual, because of widened cognitive ability, relies more on the mind and, as a result, is characterized by planned behavior which increases the individual's proficiency.

Formal-Operational Processes

Abstract Reasoning. The thinking processes of adolescents begin to resemble conceptually those of adults because the individual can do relatively complex abstract reasoning. The formal individual is able, for example, to carry on a whole series of mental, logical processes using operations. She can hold a large body of information in her mind and perform several mental manipulations on it. It is precisely this *mental holding power* and the acting on and interrelating of what is held that demarcates the formal child from those in the less cognitively developed stages, and explains why the child begins to comprehend legalistic, logical-mathematical thinking and complex literary criticism.

Hypothetical-Deductive Thinking. Formal thinkers are characterized, furthermore, by hypothetical-deductive and propositional thinking. When confronted with a problem, they formulate guesses or hypotheses and then deduce conclusions from them. For example, an adolescent might think, "The way to get a car is to ask my folks for the money. No, they won't give it to me." (An hypothesis is constructed and then rejected.) "I will have to get the money myself." (Another hypothesis is proposed.) "It, therefore, follows that I shall have to get a job and save the money for it." (A deductive operational process is used.)

Syllogistic Reasoning. The syllogism is a special case of hypothetical-deductive thinking. An example of one follows:

a. Mammals nurse their young.
b. This animal nurses its young.
c. Therefore it is a mammal.

Formal thinkers can also evaluate whether or not syllogisms are likely to be true:

a. Dogs bark.
b. This animal barked.
c. Therefore it is a dog.

Formal thinkers realize that the premise "Dogs bark" may not be sufficient because other animals may also bark.

"It therefore follows that" is a key operation involved in hypothetical-deductive thinking and identifies an advancement over the lower stage of mental development. Because formal thinkers do evaluate their conclusions, their mentality expands tremendously. Piaget believes that for individuals to have a concept of an object, (a mental process in itself), they must act mentally on it or transform it. The ability to perform operations on operations, such as checking the validity of the premise above, enables formal thinkers to further broaden their conceptualizations and perceive problems from various vantage points enabling better resolution of them.

Propositional Thinking. The adolescent may express a series of hypotheses in propositional form and reason as follows:

It is this or that.
It is this and that.
It is this but not that.
It is neither this nor that.

Or she might perform the following logical propositions:

If A then B
e.g., If it is raining (A) then the sidewalks are wet (B).
If B then A
e.g., If the sidewalks are wet, then it is raining.
Not A then Not B
e.g., If it is not raining then the sidewalks are not wet.
Not B then Not A
e.g., If the sidewalks are not wet then it is not raining.

The formal individual can relate any of the four propositions in her mind and, by reasoning, act on them to eliminate the nonappropriate ones. The individual may also hold one factor constant while varying the others. Doing this type of if-then thinking easily demarcates the formal child from those of other stages.

Conceiving of Utopia and Accepting Assumptions. The formal-operational child thinks of things not in her presence. For example, she can think of and describe an idealistic society. In addition, she can accept assumptions in solving problems. She can imagine an experiment not actually before her and describe its outcome, just as she can understand imaginary numbers.

The formal thinker also accepts assumptions for the sake of an argument, even if they are contrary to fact. A concrete-operational child will not do this. For example, if you say to a concrete child, "If bridges were made of glass . . . ," the child will probably say, "That's silly because bridges are not made of glass" or some other similar remark, indicating she does not accept your statement. The concrete child is bound to the real world and, therefore, does not make conjectures. On the contrary, formal adolescents do perform abstract thinking.

Comprehending Allegory. During the latter part of the formal period children begin to grasp double meanings in literature. For example, they are able to interpret *Gulliver's Travels* as more than just an adventure story. They also understand part-whole relationships better during this period. For example, they realize that reading a word, a line, or a sentence at a time may not result in comprehension of the author's message. The ideas have to be mentally combined and considered as a whole.

Reflexive Thinking. Reflexive thinking is one of the main processes characterizing a formal-operational child. The child at this stage is able to do this type of reasoning because she can hold more information in the mind and perform operations on it. For example, the formal adolescent can solve the following problem:

Bob is fairer than John; John is fairer than Bruce.
Who is the darkest of these?

To do this, the adolescent must perform several operations such as:

(BOB)	is fairer than	(JOHN)
(JOHN)	is fairer than	(BRUCE)
Therefore, (BOB)	is fairer than	(BRUCE)

In order to resolve the problem the child has to reflect over a series of operations and identify their functions in the thinking process. In higher mathematics, a person does essentially the same thing, as indicated below:

1. Notes the type of problem given.
2. Determines what was known and what was unknown.
3. Outlines the steps (operations) required to determine the unknown.
4. Performs the operation mentally, and sometimes with the aid of pencil and paper.

The intelligent student who has discovered her formalistic mind also performs reflexively after solving the problem by reviewing the operations performed, so that in the future, when presented with similar problems, she can easily determine their solution.

An example of reflexive thinking in science occurs when a student reflects over an experiment in an effort to determine better ways to obtain more accurate data. Writers and artists perform similar functions when they critically evaluate their work in an effort to convey better their ideas. The use of reflexive thought in this manner obviously contributes considerably to the caliber of work produced by students and separates them from lower academic individuals.

Combinatorial Logic. Formal-operational individuals are capable of performing combinatorial logic. This means they will use all possible combinations or factors related to a problem in solving it. For example, a student is presented with four jars containing colorless and odorless liquids. She is shown that a flask with some of these liquids plus a drop from another container labeled *g* will turn yellow. The student is then asked to attempt to duplicate the formation of the yellow solution and determine the role of each of the solutions. In order to solve the problem, the formal individual must systematically go about combining various solutions and noting the effects of each. This problem is complicated since only one of the solutions plus *g* will turn yellow, and one of the other solutions will negate this reaction.

Proportional Thinking. Formal-operational individuals, even though they have not had instruction, are able to understand and determine answers to proportion and ratio problems. For example, when given a lever problem, as indicated

PROPORTIONAL THINKING

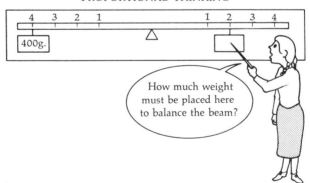

How much weight must be placed here to balance the beam?

in the illustration, they are able to determine the answer. Chemistry problems often require proportional thought. For example: The burning of carbon (from wood or coal) is $C + O_2 \rightarrow CO_2 \uparrow$. How much CO_2 will be produced if 20 grams of carbon is totally burned?

Although Piaget indicates that the ability to do proportions and ratios is achieved between eleven and fourteen, other researchers have found that this often occurs much later for many adolescents. Karplus and Peterson determined that many high school seniors cannot resolve problems of this nature.[1]

[1] R. Karplus and R. W. Peterson, "Intellectual Development Beyond Elementary School II: Ratio, A Survey," *School Science and Mathematics* 70 (December 1970): 816–18.

Controlling Variables. Formal thinkers realize that in solving a complex experimental problem they must be able to control all factors and change only one variable at a time in order to determine how it influences the reaction. An activity to determine whether children can perform this cognitive function involves presenting them with a pendulum problem. Various weights are given to them. They are asked to determine which variable affects the frequency (the number of round trip swings per minute) of the pendulum. They can vary the length of the string and weights. Concrete-operational children usually vary both variaables, length of the string and the weights, simultaneously, while formal thinkers isolate one variable at a time. They may keep the same weight on the string, swing it, and determine its frequency for a number of different lengths. In other words, they keep the weight constant while they vary the length.

Establishing Hierarchical Classification System. As seen previously, children grow significantly in their classificational abilities in the preoperational and concrete-operational stages. This continues further in the formal period when individuals are capable of establishing criteria for a hierarchical classification system. They are capable of building keys similar to those in botany, zoology, a library catalogue system, etc., in order to identify or locate a specific organism or object.

Questioning Authority and Accepting Decision by Consensus. Until late in the preoperational stage, young children tend to think that the way they perceive things is the way they are. In the late preoperational and early concrete-operational period, they rely on the views of authority figures. The way their parents, teachers, etc., see things is the way they are. At about the beginning of adolescence, this outlook changes again to a realization that rules, etc., can be determined by consensus. In addition, the moral judgment of these individuals tends to be less extreme and more accurate. To young children, a good man is totally good. For example, Dick Tracy of the comics is 100 percent good. But a formal adolescent accepts the fact that a good man may have some faults. Parents and teachers are often surprised when children at this age suddenly point out inadequacies in people.

Because of this democratic ethical development, adolescents are prone to criticize rules and family authority. This occurs because they are more likely to look at the assumptions underlying decisions. They become, as a result, much more argumentative. Parent and teachers who continue to interact with formal thinkers in authoritative ways rather than through democratic processes are likely to experience increased aggression from them. Parents need to work with children on a problem, discuss it, and help them reason to a conclusion rather than saying such things as: "You will do this because I say so."

Idealistic Egocentrism

How children perceive authority is to a large degree related to their egocentric orientation. Formal adolescents develop *idealistic egocentrism.* This is an over belief in their newly discovered rational processes. Because formal adolescents are capable of using their minds to better reason about ethics, mores, values, etc., they tend to believe that whatever they think should be that way in reality. They fail to consider what is realistically rather than idealistically possible. For example, students might reason that the United States produces more food than it needs; therefore, the excess should be given to the rest of the world. They fail to consider the problems of the political aspects involved in dealing with foreign nations. Piaget believes that employment especially helps to reduce egocentric idealism, allowing for the thinking of the individual to become more *realistically* oriented.

Time and Space

The understanding of time and space increases significantly during the formal-operational period. The adolescent thinks of distant places and larger and larger units of space. She also thinks more of imagining long periods of time. The formal-operational thinker also grasps the meaning of infinity, historical time, global geography, and interplanetary space. She can conceive of problems caused by changes in today's world.

Varied Reasoning Achievement

Because of the significant advances in operational ability during this period, formal thinkers are capable of understanding, constructing and applying abstract theories. And if what Benjamin Disraeli said is true, "A man without a theory is doomed to make the same mistakes twice," the consequence of theoretical ability is significant. Theoretical reasoning enables the individual to more effectively interact with the environment. However, adolescents vary considerably in their attempts at thinking. Kohlberg has come to the conclusion that many adults never achieve a high level of moral and formalistic development. He says, "About half of the adult American population fully reaches Piaget's stage of formal-operational reasoning and only 5 percent reach the highest moral stage."[2] To become adult in thought processes is difficult. For example, many adolescents avoid thinking critically, as if to do so were to have dire consequences or demean their intellect and "self-concept." They appear to avoid cognitive challenge and tend to want to remain in the comparative comfort of the concrete stage. Others, presumably because of more success in school or genetic and environmental differences, confront formal tasks with great tenacity, for example, higher mathematics. This is not to say that it is easy for them. It usually isn't. Present a problem requiring propositional or hypothetical-deductive thought and watch their "body language." Many of them figet, grimace, or frown as they force their mind to perform the operations required. The result of such discomfort is a broadened intellect and the attainment of greater humanness.

Summary

By attaining formal thought, the child passes through the intellectual gateway to adulthood. In doing reflexive, hypothetical-deductive, and propositional thinking, the formal adolescent is able to better use her mind to interact more effectively with both the physical and social environment.

---

[2] Lawrence Kohlberg and Rochelle Mayer, "Development as the Aim of Education," *Harvard Educational Review* 42 (4) (1972): 486.

Unfortunately, research indicates many adolescents and adults never fully reach this level. Kohlberg states that approximately 50 percent of the adult population includes fully functional formal thinkers. This means half of the adults never reach their total human potential. If this is the case, parents, teachers, and others involved in the educational process need to become aware of Piaget's theory and how to translate it into action. To do so is to insure that the reservoir of human intellect will magnify to better resolve personal as well as global problems. To fail in this pursuit is to doom many to living at an inferior level of human existence. How to facilitate formal thought is outlined in Chapter 8, "Suggestions for Teaching."

Cognitive Achievements

Listed below is a summary of the major cognitive achievements the child manifests by the end of the formal-operational period. Review it and picture how an individual behaves when she demonstrates each of these characteristics. By acting on the information in this way, you should better comprehend and retain the characteristics of the formal-operational stage.

1. Hypothetical-deductive thinking: it therefore follows that . . .
2. Propositional thinking: it is either this or that
3. Reflexive thinking: evaluating thinking processes and thinking about their thinking
4. Imagining idealistically: can think of utopia
5. Abstract thinking: no longer requires objects
6. Conceptual thinking: thinks of conceptual schemes or large, encompassing generalizations
7. Performing second-order operations: thinking of thoughts or theories
8. Mentally representing operations and operating on them: A can be greater or less than B; and if it is greater or less than C then . . .
9. Accepting contrary-to-fact assumptions: coal is white, if people were always good
10. Devising, testing, and controlling one variable at a time in an experiment
11. Performing combinational logic: Combining or eliminating elements and factors including those that do and those that do not affect a situation
12. Using proportions and ratios where applicable
13. Syllogistic reasoning: Men have beards. This person has a beard, *therefore,* he is a man.
14. Understanding and using probability
15. Establishing criteria and constructing a hierarchical classification system
16. Creating theories
17. Broadening space concept to the universe
18. Thinks of time and (past and present) and explaining infinity
19. Questioning ethics: believing they should be determined through consensus, not authority
20. Realizing thought is flexible
21. Establishing own ideals

Go to MEDIAPAK D. When you have completed it, turn to Chapter 13 in this text. Your knowledge will be reinforced by administering interviews to at least two formal-operational–aged children. Record your results as indicated by the interview form at the end of that chapter. You might also like to give some paper-and-pencil items from the "Logical Reasoning Test" in Appendix B.

General
Implications of
Piaget's Theory 7

The Need to Apply Piaget's Theory

Piaget and his colleagues have devoted their energies to determining how the mind evolves from infancy into adult maturity. They have given us great insights into cognitive development. Others must determine effective ways to apply this knowledge. Piaget has often been asked to apply his theory. He generally resists doing this, preferring to use his energies for further research. Nevertheless, he has made some suggestions for behavioral scientists and educators, which are relevant to his theory.

However, numerous investigations into the application of Piaget's theory in order to determine its use are needed. For example, how will a child be affected if parents interact with him according to his stage of development and if curriculum materials are adapted appropriately in school? We have some evidence already that there will be a positive effect. Therefore, parent-teacher training programs and curriculum materials need to be constructed to find the most appropriate ways of helping our children develop cognitively. This we are not now doing as effectively as we could be.

Parents and teachers are concerned with the total person and not just the logical-mathematical aspects of his being as outlined by Piaget. However, few will argue against the desirability of an individual's developing his cognitive abilities, and Piaget's work gives us guidance here. Through his research, we are given new perceptions of the educational environment. By looking at his investigations, evaluating and utilizing them, we should be better able to translate their implications effectively to our ends.

Today educators are increasingly being called upon to justify what is being done in the schools. Many individuals are questioning the relevance of the present curricula for today's world. The knowledge explosion demands that educators survey information to determine its worth. Evaluating knowledge for this generation to learn is no small task. No longer can we just repeat the curricula of our forefathers—Latin, Chaucer, Shakespeare, etc.—without asking the question, Is learning this material as important as studying something else, for example, population control? Regardless of the specific subject matter material selected from the banks of knowledge, the development of cognitive ability remains one of the most important tasks for school and parents to engender. Relevancy certainly must include having students learn how to use their minds in rational ways. Many school systems have already accepted this viewpoint as one of their major goals and are implementing programs to stimulate the development of cognitive ability. The work of Piaget and other cognitive psychologists has been instrumental in making educators more aware of this need. As Piaget's research becomes more widely known and understood by school personnel, the likelihood of greater efforts to provide for cognitive development undoubtedly will have more of an impact on the world's educational institutions.

There are adults who have a child's mind yet no physical evidence of brain damage. Why? What caused their mental deficiency? How could it have been prevented? What can be done to change those so afflicted? We do not yet know the answers to these questions. They must be answered by behavioral scientists, clinical psychologists, psychiatrists, guidance counselors, educators, parents, teachers, etc., who perhaps will employ Piaget's theory in answering these questions.

Further applications and the testing of Piaget's theory will come. The implications of his work are as diverse as people are complex, for their complexity radiates from their minds. In this chapter are tentatively enumerated only a few of those applications I believe most salient. As you become more versed in Piaget's theory, others will undoubtedly come to mind because of your own life experiences.

The Child's Mind, Not the Adult's Mind

When parents and teachers become aware of Piaget's theory and administer some of his tasks to children, they are usually shocked to find that a child's mind is not adult's. Subsequently, they better comprehend that children do not perceive or think as adults, and they soon grasp that the mind slowly evolves through a definite sequence. The typical adult often interacts with children as though they were capable of performing sophisticated operations. Piagetian-oriented adults do not make such assumptions. They know children's thinking processes are not similar to theirs and, as a consequence, do not require children to perform mental tasks beyond their capabilities. They interact with children by applying Piaget's theory and thus prove a less frustrating psychological environment.

Memorizing vs. Reasoning

If parents force a child to perform operations beyond his capability, they may cause detrimental effects. For example, a concrete-operational child demanded to give a formal-operational response will be unable to reason an answer. The child, as a result, will fall back on his memory and learn to distrust his thinking ability. Children like this may soon learn that it is better not to think and, in fact, may often refuse to think. When confronted with a new type of mathematical problem, they guess at its answer or state they do not know how to work the problem. They expend little effort in trying to reason. For example, they do not ask themselves: What is the nature of the problem? What is known or unknown about it? As students, they memorize formulas without understanding them. If asked what will happen to a portion of a formula if a number is increased in one part of it, they do not know until they actually work out the problem. If they are asked to explain the relations between the parts of the formula, they are at a loss. Unfortunately, this type of individual, the "memory relier" is found in every classroom from the early elementary to the university level.

Teachers and parents in the past have greatly influenced the development of memorizers instead of sophisticated, rational individuals. Szent-Gyorgyi, the renowned scientist, has questioned the overemphasis on this type of memorizing. He suggests, as Piaget, that the emphasis on memorization at the expense of thinking may actually impede the development of higher levels of reasoning. Children's habituation to relying on recognitional and evocational memory responses often has occurred because adults have not understood cognitive development or the role of reconstructive memory. In the light of Piaget's research, recognitional and evocational emphasis at the expense of operational, reconstructional abilities certainly is open to serious questioning. It is important, therefore, that adults comprehend the various memory abilities and the stages of mental development so that they can interact appropriately with children to enhance, not hinder, their cognitive abilities.

Equilibration Takes Time

The process of equilibration explains why a person bothers to think or become rational. Piaget believes the equilibration process is the driving force that causes an individual to move from one level to a higher level of cognitive development. Little can be done directly to influence the equilibration process. However, the social and physical environment indirectly influences it and can be modified to enhance or deprive it. A rich environment plays a major role in the manifestation of cognitive ability because it is more likely to present disequilibrium, thus forcing the mind to accommodate information and formulate new schemes.

Comprehension of the equilibration process by parents and teachers should give them more direction in their interaction with children. We Americans are raised in an efficiency-oriented environment. We are confronted with problems and devise methods for resolving them. This cultural behavior permeates our relations with children. We give them information and expect an almost immediate response or change in their behavior. But, assimilation and accommodation take time. We should not be impatient with our children as they perform these functions. It should be remembered that a child may be involved in some activity today, the accommodation of which may not occur until some time in the future when the child has had further experiences. These experiences may give sufficient additional data to make the accommodation process possible. If this is so, children should be allowed time to "mess around." Psychological and educational research, as yet, has not determined to the satisfaction of all how important such activity may be in cognitive development, but it seems reasonable. Some time devoted to unstructured, educational activities is warranted and probably has desirable ramifications, especially for the young primary children.

Teachers and parents should also be careful in giving names to things or processes before the child has had a chance to accommodate their meaning. To do so may stop the equilibration process. For example, when a teacher says, "That occurs because of air pressure," the child may stop observing or thinking about what is occurring because he has a name for the process. Names should come after a child comprehends what is going on.

Bertrand Russell has noted that he has required extensive periods of time to solve certain mathematical problems. After working on them for a lengthy period without success, he gave their resolution up and turned to other activities only to come back several months later with better insights into how to attack them. He called this span of time when he was not involved in solving the problem the *incubation period* because, even though he was not directly working on solving them, his mind apparently was incubating ideas.

Piaget's research suggests that children, too, occasionally need time to incubate ideas in order to accommodate them.

Adults Are Influential

It has already been pointed out that a rich, discriminating environment contributes heavily to the manifestation of cognitive development. Central to this environment are the adults surrounding the child. They provide much of the nourishment for the child's mind. A mind without *operational* food, just as a body without nutrients, does not grow well.

The Harvard Pre-School Project started in 1965 by Dr. Burton L. White gives some evidence for this view.[1] This group found, in assessing children's intellectual competence at ages three and six, that they could relatively easily identify very competent children from those less able. Furthermore, the competent children of age three differed little in performing most tasks from the older competent children of age six. They concluded from this initial research that the foundation of this competence must have developed before age three.

The staff set about studying in detail with tape recorders children's interactions in their homes. They found there is a critical period between ten and eighteen months. If a child does not receive the proper input during this period, he will be less likely to manifest high intellectual abilities. In this study, competent children came from homes where there was a variety of toys and household objects available to them. They also had considerable freedom to roam about the house. Because these mothers allowed such freedom, they were usually not as good housekeepers as the mothers of less competent children. The less competent children's mothers often restricted them and placed much of the house out of

---

[1] Maya Pines, "A Child's Mind Is Shaped before Age 2," *Life*, Dec. 17, 1971, pp. 63–67.

bounds. Competent mothers also differed in the attention they gave their children. They paused more frequently to talk to them and interacted more through language and game-type activities. They usually did this in short twenty to thirty second periods of time.

As a result of his research, White believes, like Piaget, that action is so important to the child's cognitive development that the use of playpens, high chairs, gates, and other restrictive devices should be severely curtailed.

Furthermore, psychological research has found that usually the first child is the most intelligent. This superiority of the first born compared to other children cannot be explained by genetics. Each child in a family, genetically speaking, has the same possibility for being as intelligent as any other child. If this is so, then why is it that the first born often seems more intelligent? Piaget has pointed out the importance of social interaction in nurturing mental development. The first born has almost the total attention of his parents. They are often fascinated with their offspring and devote much of their attention to him. However, as more children enter the family group, the attention and the fascination of the parents with the children often decreases. In a sense, the second child is likely to have less interaction with his parents. The result is that there is less adaptive pressure requiring him to accommodate information from his environment. The mind only develops by having opportunities to equilibrate—less stimulation of the right type means less or slower development.

Therefore, the importance of parents' spending time with their children is paramount. Feynam, a brilliant physicist, has emphasized this point in his own development. He believes that much of his intellectual ability can be traced to his father. When a child, Feynam's father often took him on nature walks or visits to museums and other places of interest. Although not formally well educated, his father knew enough to ask his son questions to stimulate his thinking. For example, one day young Feynam saw a bird and asked his father its name. The elder Feynam replied, "It's not so important that you know the name of a bird, but that you observe it—notice its wings, beak, legs, and food-gathering habits vary from other birds." What the father was doing was suggesting that the young boy compare birds in his mind. For the child to do this, he had to observe birds, analyze how they vary, and relate structures with functions. Certainly, knowing the name of a bird provided little food for thought compared to understanding its many adaptations. Feynam's father provided mental stimulation through the questions he asked, opening broad vistas for his son's mind.

It is often assumed by educators and adults that the school is the primary force in building children's minds. Although the school does play a decided role, its effect is not as great as people believe, particularly for the cognitive levels below formal, as has been already pointed out. A child spends a minor part of his life in the formalized setting of the school. Of 365 days, he spends approximately 180 in class. And, in a twenty-four hour day, only about five hours are spent in academic learning. The rest of the day and the year, his nonschool environment influences him. To think that the school has a major effect on the individual when he spends so much more time out of school is questionable. The Plowden Commission in England, in assessing the variance in achievement of eleven year olds, found that only one-third of such variance could be attributed to the school.[2]

Therefore, the home and community environments are usually the major forces in educating and establishing a value for education. If the home respects and admires the child and if there are adult models depicting the advantages of an education, the child will accommodate these values and have a good attitude toward learning, which in turn better affects his achievements.[3] The importance of adults in providing the intellectual stimulus the child needs during the sensory-motor and preoperational stages cannot be underrated. If a child does not have a positively stimulating human environment during these periods, he will be intellectually behind before he ever starts school. Operation Head Start was founded on the assumption that early childhood development is extremely important in the progression of cognitive development. This program reasoned that if a child has a firm cognitive foundation during the early periods he will be better able to accommodate the educational program of the school.

Although the research to substantiate Head Start is equivocal, there is some evidence to show that it can be effective, providing it is specifically designed to enhance cognitive development. Louis T. DiLorenzo, Director of the Research Training Program in the Department of Educational Research, State University College at Brockport, New York, did a four-year study of the prekindergarten programs for the disadvantaged in New York and found that structured academic, cognitive programs were the most successful. In conclusion, he reported, "Cognitively oriented programs produced significantly greater results than traditional nursery education programs in developing language skills and increasing IQ scores.[4]

Early Reading Emphasis

The American schools emphasize learning to read. Instruction in most schools during the entire year is reading centered. As a result, there is a rush to get a child to read as soon as possible. The first grade teacher usually feels she has failed if children under her care do not meet reading objectives for that grade. In fact, the first grade teacher really has a responsibility to insure that the first grader does read because the second grade instruction is dependent upon at least first grade reading ability, and so it goes on up the educational ladder.

There is much to be said for delaying the emphasis on reading, particularly in the primary years. Many of the English infant schools, for example, do not rush children to read. These children enter the primary school within a few months of their fifth birthday and are placed with other children of varying ages in nonformalized learning environments. They stay in these schools for several

[2] Kenneth Lovell, "Some Problems Associated with Formal Thought and Its Assessment," in *Measurement and Piaget*, eds. Donald R. Green, Margerite P. Ford, and George B. Flamer (New York: McGraw-Hill, 1971), p. 88.

[3] Torsten Husen, "Does More Time in School Make a Difference?" *Saturday Review*, April 29, 1972, pp. 32–35.

[4] Louis T. DiLorenzo, "Which Way for Pre-K: Wishes or Reality?" *American Education*, January-February 1971, p. 30.

years. Their teachers, as a consequence, have considerable time to develop the children's reading competence and do not feel any great need to have their pupils become early readers. Children in these schools learn to read when they are ready.

There is evidence that visual maturity also varies among children. Luella Cole found some children cannot fixate on objects that are close until they are seven or eight.[5] Ruth Strang, Homer Carter, and Dorothy McGinnis found that when children are unable to adjust to tasks requiring close vision, such as reading, they just give up trying to do them.[6]

If instruction in American schools were to become less reading dependent and utilize more audio-visual aids, such as, tapes, 35 mm slides, etc., learning to read could be delayed. Marshall McCluhan has pointed out that children today are more knowledgeable because of the advent of technology—radio, T.V., movie pictures, etc.—than from reading.[7] Yet, the schools are still shackled with the overemphasis on the importance of reading.

Making young children read words without understanding their meaning is a questionable educational practice. A preoperational child, for example, often has to mouth words in a text requiring concrete-operational thought. The child certainly will not be able to comprehend such passages. Before a child will be able to read with understanding, he must be able to seriate, classify, and perform other logical operations. Careful analyses of reading material for children should be made to see if it is beyond their experience and operational abilities. A child reading material beyond his operational level of comprehension may develop detrimental reading attitudes. He may believe reading is not enjoyable, is meaningless, and is a chore to be done at the demand of the teacher, but certainly not one he would want to perform if he had a choice.

The noted child psychologist Millie Almy believes there is a close relationship between reading attainment and cognitive development. She says:

> Language is important, but for Piaget the ability to use language to express logic is an outcome of activity. Attempts to improve the child's logic solely through instructing him in the use of language are not likely to be very successful. . . .
>
> The findings in our studies of a rather substantial correlation between performance in conservation tasks and progress in beginning reading suggests that, to some extent, similar abilities are involved. A program designed to nurture logical thought should contribute positively to readiness for reading.[8]

Reading experts, therefore, need to consider whether it might be more effective and efficient to adjust learning to read until a child is well into the concrete-operational period. This would better insure that the reading material is within his experiential background and operational level of understanding.

---

[5] Luella Cole, *The Improvement of Reading, with Special Reference to Remedial Instruction* (New York: Holt, Rinehart and Winston, 1938).

[6] Ruth Strang, *Diagnostic Teaching of Reading* (New York: McGraw-Hill, 1964), pp. 164–65.

[7] Marshall McCluhan, *The Medium Is the Message: An Inventory of Effects* (New York: Bantam Books, 1967).

[8] Millie Almy, *Young Children's Thinking* (New York: Teacher's College Press, 1966).

If a child has a propensity and a desire to read, he should certainly be encouraged, but, if the opposite is the case, it may well be desirable to delay reading emphasis.

Early Schooling Questioned

There is an increasing concern about providing early schooling for children. Elkind, in reacting to many educators emphasizing earlier schooling, suggests that formalized instruction may be far more effective if it were delayed until children were eight years old. He reasons from research done by Bloom, indicating that a child only has about 50 percent of his intellectual ability by age four and about 80 percent by age eight, that a child could more easily learn at eight and not have to unlearn poor habits, attitudes, etc. Studies done in Europe do give some credence to Elkind's suggestions. The International Association in Educational Achievement (IEA) has performed a series of massive studies investigating school effectiveness in several countries. Some nations require school attendance beginning at five, for example, Scotland and England, while others delay until age seven, for example Sweden and Finland. The IEA found that children entering school systems at six perform mathematically significantly better at age fourteen than do children entering school at five.[9]

Raymond S. Moore, Robert D. Moon, and Dennis R. Moore in an extensive review of anatomical, physiological, psychological, and educational research on early schooling concluded:

> It would be hard to find an area of educational research more definitive than that on child development and school entry age. It is difficult to see how planners can review this evidence and conclude that four or five-year-olds generally should be in school much less than three-year-olds. . . . Meanwhile, scientific evidence comparing the validity of the home and the school as early childhood environment clearly favors the home.[10]

What Is a Good Learning Environment?

Piaget believes children should be actively involved in the learning process. They should be confronted with novel and interesting situations. He has reiterated on several occasions, "There is no learning without experience." By this, he means there is only as much meaning behind a word or thing as a child has had experience with it. Young children, therefore, need to encounter their environment through activity. These encounters should be almost entirely with things and people during the sensory-motor, preoperational, and early concrete-operational levels. This is not to say that active involvement is not also desirable in the formal stage, but the use of pictorial and symbolic language may play a greater role at this level.

---

[9] Husen, "Does More Time . . . ," p. 32.

[10] Raymond S. Moore, Robert D. Moon, and Dennis R. Moore, "The California Report: Early Schooling for All?" *Phi Delta Kappan*, June 1972, p. 621.

Essentially, Piaget's work implies instruction should be student centered rather than teacher centered. This viewpoint arises from an understanding of the assimilation and accommodation process. A parent or teacher may provide information, but, once children have this information, they should be required to act upon it to insure that they internalize it and that it becomes ingested into their schemes. For example, an eighth grade science teacher may have students developing a conceptual understanding about a cold air front moving in over an area and then ask the children to construct a metaphor or analogy to describe what happens. A student might come up with, "A cold front is like a bucket of cold water. The cold water may move in. When it pours down, the environment is changed, and you are suddenly made cold." This example clearly illustrates the child has some comprehension of fronts. It further indicates that he has assimilated and accommodated information about them because he would not be able to formulate an analogy of this type unless he had done so.

Learning

Piaget believes a child learns what he is cognitively capable of learning. In other words, development explains learning. Some psychologists argue with this view. They think mental development will follow if a child learns a series of items in sequence. Once he has mastered these, he will achieve the desired level of mental ability. In other words, mental development can be accelerated providing the right competencies are identified for the child to learn in the right order. The sequencing of learning activity without taking into account the child's stage of mental development may be disputed because psychologists have not yet done sufficient research in the area, particularly with young children. Furthermore, there is no evidence as yet to show that programmed instruction accelerates the passage from one cognitive level to another.

Piaget has assumed in his research that all children have had similar random experiences or inputs. This assumption was necessary in order for him to produce general statements about children of different age groups. The concept of readiness is based upon this assumption of randomness. Essentially, his reasoning is as follows:

1. All children have had similar experiences.
2. They should, therefore, develop reasonably (assuming no cerebral or genetic differences) at about the same rate.
3. If this is so, then parents or educators should consider the stage of development (readiness) before requiring certain tasks.

Some psychologists, for example, Jerome Bruner and Robert Gagné, disagree with this idea of the similarity of encounter of children and, therefore, do not accept Piaget's concept of readiness. Bruner believes almost anything can be taught at any age, provided it is adjusted to the level of competence of the child and the material is presented in an interesting and understandable manner. Gagné believes that, if the proper sequence of learning materials is determined and administered to the child, he can learn the concepts involved.

Piaget, on the other hand, believes that there is a generalized system operating within the mind involved in assimilating and accommodating information. This system increasingly becomes more sophisticated as a child develops. Piaget agrees that you might accelerate the learning of a concept, for example, of conservation, but questions whether or not you should attempt to achieve what he considers the American wish for accelerating mental development. Americans are usually trying to do something faster, more efficiently, and effectively and American educators are no exception. Since, to Piaget, it is the entire mental system that seems to progress through mental development, the training of children on one small part of that system will have little lasting or valuable effect. He says in this respect:

> Acceleration is certainly possible, but first we must find out whether it is desirable or harmful. Take the concept of object permanency—the realization that a ball, a rattle, or a person continues to exist when it no longer can be seen. A kitten develops this concept at four months, a human baby at nine months; but the kitten stops right there while the baby goes on to learn more advanced concepts. Perhaps a certain slowness is useful in developing the capacity to assimilate new concepts.[11]

He suggests that rather than trying to accelerate learning, parents and teachers should provide children with rich experiences at their stage of development. This means an instructor should endeavor to determine a child's stage of development and adjust learning activities for his ability. Thus, evaluational tests need to be developed to determine what a child is cognitively capable of doing, and then much of the instruction designed for him would have to be individualized.

Readiness, according to Piaget, appears to encompass a broad number of mental strategies and should be thought of as a complex of capabilities. Whether Piaget, Bruner, or Gagné are correct in their viewpoints can only be resolved after extensive further research.

Piagetian Tests More Diagnostic

Related to Piaget's concept of readiness is intelligence. Intelligence generally is measured by IQ tests. Traditionally, IQ tests have been designed along pragmatic lines. The psychologist constructed a series of questions and gave these questions to children. If the majority of children managed to get them right at a certain age, say ten and above, these items were thought to indicate a mental age of at least ten. IQ is defined as the mental age over the chronological age. However, the problem with the traditional IQ test is that it has no theoretical basis except trial and error. Hardi Fischer in reviewing intelligence tests says:

> Most of the well-known intelligence tests are too verbal, also containing numerical tasks, or they depend on scholastic performance. Piaget's experi-

---

[11] Elizabeth Hall, "A Conversation with Jean Piaget and Barbel Inhelder," *Psychology Today*, May 1970, p. 31.

ments, when used clinically, present a broader situation than these tests. In tests you have mostly a sort of performance to judge, but you don't know the underlying reasoning processes. Piaget's experiments give this information and they also permit an evaluation of educability.[12]

It is apparent that Piaget's theoretical model could be used to construct a test to assess cognitive development. Piaget views intelligence as the continued process of adaptation and organization of inputs by the child's mind as he interacts with the environment. An indication of the sophistication of the child's intelligence is his ability to perform certain operational tasks. Piaget does not consider intelligence as being a fixed potential as is usually the case when the term is used with traditional IQ tests. He prefers to think of intelligence as being a progressive evolutionary process. For example, one child might perform concrete-operational tasks before another, only to be surpassed by the slower child at a later time in development. Piaget, as well as other researchers, has shown that the rate of learning varies with development. The younger child takes much longer to learn even a simple task than do children in more advanced stages. Therefore, the nature of the task and the ease of performance give insights into the child's capabilities. Piagetian-oriented intelligence tests, unlike traditional IQ tests, have diagnostic value and do not carry with them the "value" component of traditional IQ tests; for example, 150 IQ is better than 100 IQ. The use of traditional IQ tests occasionally has crippling effects on students who are told that their IQ scores are below average. Such information may contribute to poor self-concepts in these students.

Piagetian types of intelligence tests merely assess the cognitive ability of the child. Piaget believes there is a hierarchical basis of intelligence. Each level of intelligence is followed by another, more sophisticated, one. Decaré found in her research evidence to substantiate this view. In constructing an *object permanence task* evaluational instrument, she found that sensory-motor children never passed an advanced stage above the one they failed. She also found in studying ninety children that the conclusions Piaget reached after studying his three children were supported by her investigations.[13]

However, Tuddenham has tried without success over several years to develop a test to be used to place a child on a continuum of cognitive development. The tests he has devised differed from Decaré's in that they assessed a number of different types of operations. He states that from his research he holds little hope of ever being able to produce a test that will have high predictive value of a child's performance.[14]

Efforts have been made to construct other types of Piagetian tests. Barbel Inhelder and Vinh-Bang at the Geneva institute began work on some evaluational instruments in the 1950s. Object permanence tasks tests were devised for the

[12] Hardi Fischer, "The Psychology of Piaget and Its Educational Applications," *International Review of Education* 10 (1964) : 438.

[13] T. G. Decaré, *Intelligence and Affectivity in Early Childhood* (New York: International Press, 1965).

[14] J. Douglas Ayers, "Comments on Tuddenham's Paper," in *Measurement and Piaget*, . . . , p. 75.

sensory-motor period and conservation tasks tests were constructed for the elementary years. Each item on these tests attempts to determine the presence or absence of some cognitive ability. Unlike traditional IQ tests, a wrong answer gives as much information as a correct response. For example, if a child fails to do reversible thinking, he is not concrete-operational.

Using Piaget's findings, Laurendeau and Pinard have developed scales on realism, animism, finalism, dynamism, and artificialism for children ages four to eleven. Lyle Joyce and Paul Ankney developed a concrete-operational paper-pencil test,[15] and Gil Burney prepared a similar one for the formal-operational level.[16]

Although some Piagetian assessment measures have been developed, Elkind cautions that too much hope should not be attributed to their contribution. He argues that traditional IQ tests give a broader measure of the individuals' abilities, have better predictive value in school curricula, and are more easily used by counselors and clinicians because of their philosophical and educational backgrounds than Piagetian tests.[17] Tuddenham, however, disagrees with Elkind in that he believes Piagetian tests can be particularly helpful in assessing certain curriculum renovations.[18]

The British Psychological Society, aware of the problem in using the traditional IQ tests, has sponsored the construction of the British Intelligence Scale. It includes twelve subscales, one of which has to do with operational thinking. It is hoped that such an instrument will give a broader view of human ability than do IQ tests. The test will indicate, in addition to other abilities, whether an individual is on a preoperational, concrete-, or formal-operational level.[19]

Whether or not a similar test will be used in the United States will undoubtedly be determined by the success of the British scale. If this test or new ones are made available, a major effort will have to be made to train teachers, counselors, and guidance personnel in their philosophical basis, uses, and how to administer them. Teachers, furthermore, will have to be shown how to translate the knowledge obtained from the tests so as to adjust the learning environment for children's capabilities. At the present time, very few teachers and guidance counselors are sufficiently trained in Piagetian theory to apply it.

Designing a Curriculum for Cognitive Development

The development of curriculum in science, mathematics, etc., for elementary to secondary school aged students is an extremely complex task. Traditionally,

---

[15] Paul Ankney and Lyle Joyce, "The Development of a Piagetian Paper and Pencil Test for Assessing Concrete Operational Reasoning" (Ph.D. diss, University of Northern Colorado, 1974).

[16] Gilbert M. Burney, "The Construction and Validation of an Objective Formal Reasoning Instrument" (Ph.D. diss., University of Northern Colorado, 1974).

[17] David Elkind, "Two Approaches to Intelligence: Piagetian and Psychometric," in *Measurement and Piaget*, . . . , p. 27.

[18] Read D. Tuddenham, "Comments on Elkind's Paper," in *Measurement and Piaget*, . . . , p. 30.

[19] Thomas G. Sticht, "Comments on Kenneth Lovell's Paper: Does Learning Recapitulate Ontogeny?" in *Measurement and Piaget*, . . . , p. 93.

curricula have been constructed by adults using different philosophical bases for their organization. One approach has been to emphasize *subject matter topics* and to arrange these to follow a logical sequence. For example, in science, a sound lesson might be followed by one on light because both sound and light are wave phenomena and are, therefore, cognitively related.

Another approach has been to form a curriculum around major topics or generalizations of a discipline, the *conceptual scheme* approach. For example, in mathematics, the schemes might include properties and applications of probabilities or, in science, "matter exists in the form of units which can be classified into hierarchies of organizational levels."[20]

A more recent approach has been to use the development of *cognitive competencies* as the main skeletal structure of the curriculum. In this design, the nurturing of such abilities as measuring, observing, predicting, etc., is the basic concern. Subject matter is involved in the curriculum, but its importance is secondary to the child's learning to manifest certain of these cognitive processes. In this type of curriculum, subject matter becomes the vehicle for developing children's strategies of thought.

All of these curriculum systems are used today. However, regardless of the form of instruction, the amount of structure, or the directiveness given in the teaching of subject matter, many of the modern curricula emphasize active involvement by students.

Discovery-Inquiry Teaching

Several science, mathematics, social studies, and language arts curricula have been designed around what is called the discovery or inquiry approaches. These titles mean different things to different people, but essentially there is agreement among educators that, with this approach, the child is not told the answers to problems. The learning environment is structured to enable the child to discover through his own mental actions concepts and principles. The purpose of these approaches is to have children mediate out and internalize concepts. The role of the teacher is to set up the learning environment and act as a facilitator in helping children make discoveries. It is argued by the proponents of discovery, particulary Bruner of Harvard, that this approach has the following advantages:

1. Increase in intellectual potency.
2. Shifts from extrinsic to intrinsic rewards.
3. Helps to learn how to discover.
4. Aids in memory processing.

Bruner believes discovery learning increases intellectual potency because it forces the individual to use his mind in generating meaning. Realizing how his mind is capable of functioning, the student receives self-satisfaction—intrinsic rewards. Bruner believes that in order for individuals to want to use their minds and to continue to explore and become knowledgeable, they must have had success in doing this many times. Schools traditionally have emphasized the giving

---

[20] National Science Teachers Association, *Theory into Action in Science Curriculum Development* (Washington, D.C.: NCTA, 1964), p. 20.

of external or extrinsic rewards in the form of grades, letters, etc. These are valuable, but Bruner argues that what is really needed is to have students become aware that using their minds is exciting and important for building a person's self-concept.

The only way an individual learns to play football is to play football. Bruner believes the only way a person learns to discover is to be involved in discovering. It is, therefore, extremely important for children to have multiple opportunities to make discoveries so that they develop their human potential.

Elkind, however, questions the interpretation of Piaget's ideas to support discovery teaching as a means of stimulating intrinsic motivation. He argues that the discovery emphasis now prevalent in education is misconceived since it assumes that intrinsic motivation can be built within the materials and methods used by the instructor. He points out that Piaget insists that motivation lies within the child. The child should choose the materials appropriate to him. Elkind says:

> Without the opportunity for student choice and the provision of large blocks of time, in which the child can totally engross himself in an activity, the values of intrinsic motivation will not be realized. . . . In clinical practice we often see children (and adults) who are unwilling to form any emotional attachment. In the history of such children one always finds a series of broken relationships due to a wide variety of causes including the death of parents or the forced separation from them. Such children have learned that every time they have reached out and become emotionally involved, rejection, hurt, and misery were the result. Consequently, they prefer not to get involved any more because the pain and anguish of still another broken relationship is just too high a price to pay for an emotional attachment. The intellectually burned child is in somewhat the same position. He refuses to become totally involved in intellectual activities because the repeated frustration of being interrupted in the middle is just too much to bear. Our lockstep curricula, 30 minutes for this and an hour for that, have the consequence, I suspect, of producing intellectually burned chidren who shun the fire of intense mental involvement.
>
> Accordingly, the educational practice which would best foster intrinsically motivated children in the Piagetian and Montessori sense would be the provision of "interest areas" where children could go on their own and for long periods of time. Only when the child can choose an activity and persist at it until he is satisfied can we speak of truly intrinsically motivated behavior. Where such interest areas and time provisions have been made, as in the World of Inquiry School in Rochester, New York, the results are impressive indeed.[21]

Much of what Elkind says about interest areas has support from experimentation done in the English infant schools.[22,23] It should be noted, however, that

---

[21] Elkind, "Two Approaches . . . ," pp. 25–26. Used with permission of McGraw-Hill Book Co.

[22] Central Advisory Council for Education, *Children and the Primary Schools*, 2 vols. (London: Her Majesty's Stationery Office, 1967). It is also referred to as the Plowden Report after its chairperson, Lady Bridget Plowden.

[23] Joseph Featherstone, "Schools for Children, What's Happening in British Classrooms," *New Republic*, August 10, 1967; "How Children Learn, " *New Republic*, September 2, 1967; "Teaching Children to Think," *New Republic*, September 9, 1972.

these areas often contain discovery-oriented curriculum materials similar to those suggested by Bruner.

Although Elkind questions the possibility of building intrinsic motivation in materials and procedures, there is considerable evidence that the modern discovery or inquiry-oriented curricula have been educationally successful.

Shulman, as a result of a conference on learning by discovery, summarizes the research in discovery as follows: "In the published studies, guided discovery treatments generally have done well both at the level of immediate learning and later transfer."[24]

Similar conclusions have been found by the Biological Sciences Curriculum Study for inquiry approaches in biology,[25] by William W. Day[26] and Omar T. Henkel for Physics,[27] by John J. Montean for General Chemistry and General Science,[28] and John M. Good, John V. Farley, and Edwin Fenton in Social Studies[29] plus many others.

In respect to operational thinking, Lovell found in a review of studies on the formal level that exposure to this type of thinking was effective in aiding a student to develop formal operations after age thirteen. He also noted that knowledge of the subject and a positive attitude toward it enhanced formal thought.[30]

Harry Beilin, editor of the *Journal of Experimental Child Psychology*, made an extensive review of research related to the effects of training in logical operations. He concludes: "The data from these diverse studies show that training makes possible an improvement in performance in practically every type of logical or infralogical operation."[31]

Is planning the curriculum in the manner suggested above worth the work involved? Herbert D. Thier, the assistant director of the Science Curriculum Improvement Study, University of California, in summarizing research, came to the following conclusion. "What all of this rather new research by Piaget's associates seem to indicate is that carefully chosen curricular experiences can have a significant effect on the intellectual development of children."[32]

---

[24] Lee S. Shulman, "Psychological Controversies in the Teaching of Science and Mathematics," *Science Teacher*, September 1968, p. 90.

[25] "Evaluation," *BSCS Newsletter* 24 (January 1965).

[26] William Worthy Day, IV, "Physics and Critical Thinking: An Experimental Evaluation of PSSC and Traditional Physics in Six Areas of Critical Thinking While Controlling for Intelligence, Achievement, Course Background and Mobility by Analysis of Covariance" (Ph.D. diss., The University of Nebraska Teachers College, 1964), cited in *Dissertation Abstracts* XXV (1964): 4197.

[27] Omar Thomas Henkel, "A Study of Changes in Critical Thinking Ability: A Result of Instruction in Physics" (Ph.D. diss., The University of Toledo, 1965), cited in *Dissertation Abstracts* XXVI (1965): 5291.

[28] John J. Montean, "An Experimental Study of Discussion Groups in General Chemistry and General Science as a Means of Group Growth in Critical Thinking" (Ph.D. diss. Syracuse University, 1959), cited in *Dissertation Abstracts* XX (1959): 3666–67.

[29] John M. Good, John V. Farley, and Edwin Fenton, "Developing Inquiry Skills with an Experimental Social Studies Curriculum," *The Journal of Educational Research* (1) (September 1969): 31–35.

[30] Lovell, "Some Problems . . . ," pp. 90–91.

[31] Harry Beilin, "Piagetian and Cognitive Development Research and Mathematical Education," in proceedings of an NCTM conference conducted at Columbia University, October 1970, pp. 81–124.

[32] Herbert D. Thier, *Teaching Elementary School Science, A Laboratory Approach* (Lexington, Mass.: D. C. Heath, 1970).

Psychologists have known for years that the greater the involvement of the individual in the learning process, the more he comes to know. This involvement, however, usually has been taken to mean that the child mainly learns knowledge.

Piaget's work has contributed to a shift in this viewpoint. Involvement now means to many educators the active participation of the child in performing operations. By the child's making such an investment, there is a greater mental impact, resulting in better learning and memory retention.

Piaget's work suggests that curriculum planners should consider the following:

1. Emphasize active involvement by children and intrinsic motivation.
2. Realize experience not only includes learning about phenomena but also discovering how to use the mind.
3. Develop a curriculum so that it moves from the concrete to the abstract. This is particularly important for the elementary level. Stress situations requiring cognitive responses.
4. Do not design a curriculum so that it is sequenced or organized according to what appears to be logical to adults, but take into consideration the stages of cognitive development.
5. Attempt to diagnose children's mental capabilities and modify the curriculum so as to help them develop their cognitive abilities. The curriculum should be adjusted to the child and not the child to the curriculum.
6. Assess both the outcomes in performing operations and subject matter knowledge.

Curriculum Information Still Needed

Although the six suggestions made above may aid curriculum planners, many problems still remain unresolved. Educators need to know far more about how children learn concepts and pass from one stage of mental development to another. Before curriculum experts can enhance the movement of children from stage to stage, much more information is needed. Piaget's work does, however, give the curriculum developer some assistance by indicating how learning activities should be sequenced, and his work has revealed the importance of sequencing. Furthermore, the clinical techniques (méthode clinique) Piaget has utilized for gaining insights into the child's cognitive operations and concept formation can be used by curriculum organizers to investigate other curricular problems.

Presently, there are curriculum materials being programmed for the computer. The child responds to information fed by the computer, and his response is recorded by the machine. The curriculum builder, at the end of a trial run on a curriculum, receives feedback on how the children responded to the sequence. If a child does not have success in progressing from Step A to Step B, there must be something wrong with the way the curriculum is constructed. The planner can immediately modify the curriculum accordingly and retest its effectiveness. Unfortunately, often when curriculum planners use this system, they mainly analyze their work from a subject matter viewpoint or by a trial and error approach. The analysis of the problem from a cognitive frame of reference would better help resolve problems in sequencing. It would also assist in gaining better insights into concept formation that would be of value when working on other curriculum materials.

Gagné emphasizes the importance of analyzing and determining what children should learn, such as, skills, attitudes, and cognitive abilities. He believes this should be done so that curriculum materials can be organized to insure the manifestation of these competencies, producing better educated individuals as a result. Gagné argues that instructors will not teach for competencies nor direct efforts toward their attainment unless they are specified. The task of the curriculum director, therefore, is amplified, and the priority of stimulating cognitive development magnified. A modern curriculum must integrate the development of subject matter, basic skills, cognitive development, and operational proficiency, striving constantly to develop positive learning attitudes and affectivity. The application of Piaget's theory, while not sufficient to this purpose, can be instrumental to this end.

Piagetian-oriented Curricula

Several curricula have been developed utilizing Piaget's research as a guide in grade-placing activities and as a general basis in developing exercises requiring the use of logical-mathematical thinking.

Early Childhood Curriculum. Celia Stendler Lavatelli has experimented with and produced an early childhood curriculum which is a Piagetian-oriented program. It contains several kits containing various types of materials to use with small groups of children. These are essentially Piagetian tasks for transitional preoperational children. The purpose is to involve children in seriation; ordering; one-to-one correspondence; conservation; number, measurement, and space operations; classification; etc. For example, children who do not order well may be given several activities requiring ordering: they may order flowers, then pictures of dolls, and later umbrellas. They are not told whether their answers are right or wrong. However, specific instructions for teaching each session are outlined. The curriculum is based on the assumption that these experiences will better help children develop their operational abilities when they are ready and capable of doing so.

Elementary Science Curricula. Three elementary science curriculum projects funded by the National Science Foundation have also utilized Piaget's research in establishing their philosophy which emphasizes active student involvement and in placing their materials in certain grade levels. These projects are Science— A Process Approach, (SAPA), Science Curriculum Improvement Study, (SCIS), and the Elementary Science Study, (ESS).

The Science—A Process Approach curriculum has produced elementary science activities for grades K-6 stressing cognitive development. It is constructed in a hierarchy of processes and tasks. Achievement in the lower levels is considered necessary for achievement in the higher ones. Although Gagné, a behaviorist, contributed heavily to the organization of this curriculum, he is in agreement with Piaget in that they both believe in the hierarchical development of the human mind. For this reason, Piaget's sequence of development of certain operations was used as a guide in determining what should be included and on what grade level.

The Science Curriculum Improvement Study (SCIS) has been very instrumental in utilizing Piaget's research and in making teachers more aware of his work for similar reasons. In fact, its staff has produced films explaining Piaget's work, which are listed at the end of this book. SCIS has produced materials and activities for grades K-6. The titles of some of these units clearly indicate the Piagetian influence since the subject matter involves seriation, ordering, classification, number and measurement, relationships, etc. The following are examples:

K-3	"Material Objects"
	"Organisms"
Grade 2	"Interaction and Systems"
	"Life Cycles"
Grade 3	"Subsystems and Variables"
	"Populations"

The Elementary Science Study differs from the other curriculum projects in that it is not an organized scope and sequence curriculum but a series of units that a teacher or student may select. Bruner and Piaget had considerable influence on the ESS curriculum designers, particularly in determining the types of activities, their nature, and their grade placement. Their influence is also evident in the premise that children must have opportunities to act on materials to develop their cognitive processes. The title of some of the ESS units indicate this orientation:

"Match and Measure" (Children measure objects.)

"Tangrams" (Given several shapes, students are asked to put them together to make new shapes.)

"Primary Balancing" (Children learn about balancing and weight.)

"Eggs and Tadpoles" (Children learn about life cycles.)

The Biological Sciences Curriculum Study at the University of Colorado, under a grant from the National Science Foundation, is presently designing a curriculum for the middle school, grades six through eight, entitled, "Human Sciences for the Middle School Program." The project staff is outlining activities for students so that they are generally cognitively adjusted for their various ages. For this purpose, they have used as a basis the Piagetian stages outlined for a similar project in England called the Science 5/13 Project which is being developed at the University of Bristol School of Education. The HSMS project is mainly concerned with three cognitive areas. Grade six has activities based on stage one, grades seven and eight have fewer stage one, and more stage two and three materials. A summary of these stages outlined by the Biological Sciences Curriculum Study in Boulder, Colorado, is shown following:

Stage One, Concrete Operations, Early Stage.

In this stage, children are developing the ability to manipulate things mentally. At first this ability is limited to objects and materials that can be manipulated concretely, and even then only in a restricted way. The objectives here are concerned with developing these mental operations through exploration of concrete objects and materials—that is to say, objects and materials which, as physical things, have meaning for the child. Since older children, and even adults, prefer an introduction to new ideas and problems through concrete example and physical exploration, these objectives are suitable for all children, whatever their age, who are being introduced to certain science activities for the first time.

Stage Two, Concrete Operations, Later Stage.

In this stage, continuation of what Piaget calls the stage of concrete operations, the mental manipulations are becoming more varied and powerful. The developing ability to handle variables—for example, in dealing with multiple classification—means that problems can be solved in more ordered and quantitative ways than was previously possible. The objectives begin to be more specific to the exploration of the scientific aspects of the environment rather than to general experience, as previously. These objectives are developments of those of stage one and depend on them for a foundation. They are thought of as being appropriate for all children who have progressed from stage one and not merely for nine to eleven year olds.

Stage Three, Transition to Abstract Thinking.

This is the stage in which, for some children, the ability to think about abstractions is developing. When this development is complete, their thought is capable of dealing with the possible and hypothetical and is not tied to the concrete and to the here and now. It may take place between eleven and thirteen for some able children, for some children it may happen later, and for others it may never occur. The objectives of this stage are ones which involve development of ability to use hypothetical reasoning and to separate and combine variables in a systematic way. They are appropriate to those who have achieved most of the stage two objectives and who now show signs of ability to manipulate mentally ideas and propositions.[33]

Many Do Not Achieve Formal-Operational Ability

Although one would get the impression from reading Piaget's works that all children eventually achieve the operational abilities he outlines, research indicates that a sizeable number of students do not. Research, furthermore, shows that many American students do not achieve certain tasks until several years after the time stated by Piaget. Elkind, for example, evaluated 469 junior and senior school students in Norton High School, Norton, Massachusetts. He found large numbers of students ages 12.6 to 17.7 did not have good conceptions of quantity, and many seniors who should be well into the formal period of cognitive development, according to Piaget, still experienced difficulty in attaining abstract conceptions of volume.

John W. Renner did a study involving 588 students grades seven through twelve, sampled from the secondary schools in Oklahoma and found only 58 of

---

[33] Biological Sciences Curriculum Study, "Objective Modules for Human Science: A BSCS Multidisciplinary Program for the Middle School," mimeographed (Boulder, Colo.: BSCS, 1972), p. 2.

them were definitely formalistic on the tasks he administered. By far, the majority of the students were concrete-operational. The results of his study, based on conservation of a solid, conservation of weight, conservation of volume, the elimination of contradiction, and exclusion of irrelevant variables tasks are shown in the chart below.[34] He suggests that what is being done to develop formal operational thought in kindergarten through twelfth grade is open to serious questioning.

Score	Classification	No. of Students
0–5	Preoperational	20
6–11	Concrete-Operational	423
12–13	Post–Concrete-Operational	87
14–16	Formal-Operational	58

Ball and Sayre studied 419 seventh through twelfth grade science students, assessing their abilities in achieving five formal-operational level tasks: stick-man ratio, pendulum controlling variables, balance proportion, combining chemicals, and combinational logic and syllogisms.[35] Their work corroborated with the findings of Renner. The number achieving formal-operational ability on each task is indicated in the table below.

	% Success on Each Task			419 Students	
Task	1	2	3	4	5
	(stickman)	(pendulum)	(balance)	(beaker)	SYL
Grade *No. of Students*					
7 70	6	13	24	33	39
8 70	7	16	41	49	60
9 74	12	11	40	51	70
10 81	26	28	60	64	77
11 67	72	51	85	88	93
12 57	81	69	93	88	95
Percent:	32%	29%	55%	61%	71%

[34] John W. Renner, Donald G. Stafford, and William B. Ragan, "Research in Formal Operations," mimeographed (Norman, Okla.: University of Oklahoma, 1971), p. 6.

[35] Daniel W. Ball and Steve A. Sayre, "Relationships between Student Piagetian Cognitive Development and Achievement in Science" (Ph.D. diss., University of Northern Colorado, 1972).

Ball and Sayre further discovered that there was a significant correlation between the number of tasks performed successfully and the scholastic grades received by the students. Those who were formal obtained generally higher scholastic grades. In grades seven through ten, 94 percent and in grades eleven through twelve, 74 percent of the formal students received grades of A or B. Five formal students out of the sample did receive grades below C. However, the predictive value of these tasks did not have as much significance for grade twelve physics since there already is a higher percentage of formal students in these classes. The study further determined there was a positive correlation between the number of Piagetian tasks performed by the students and IQ.

Comparison of Junior High School Students' Grades with Their
Overall Performance on the Piagetian Task Instrument

Scholastic Grade	No. of Students Receiving	Formal Performance	Nonformal Performance	Percent Formal	Percent Nonformal
A	19	8	11	42.1	57.4
B	74	13	61	17.6	82.4
C	78	1	77	1.3	98.7
D-F	43	1	42	2.3	97.7

Comparison of Senior High School Students' Grades with Their
Overall Performance on the Piagetian Task Instrument

Scholastic Grade	No. of Students Receiving	Formal Performance	Nonformal Performance	Percent Formal	Percent Nonformal
A	51	45	6	88.2	11.8
B	78	49	29	62.8	37.2
C	55	20	35	36.4	63.6
D-F	21	4	17	19.0	81.0

The achievement of operational tasks on the elementary level further indicated considerable variation as to what students were able to do. Almy evaluated 629 second grade children to determine the number that were clearly operational on seven different tasks. She found a relatively low number of these children were able to achieve most of the tasks as indicated by a summary table (following) from her research.[36]

---

[36] Millie Almy, "Logitudinal Studies Related to the Classroom," in *Piagetian Cognitive-Development Research and Mathematical Education*, ed. Myron F. Rosskopf et al. (Washington, D.C.: National Council of Teachers of Mathematics, 1971), p. 233.

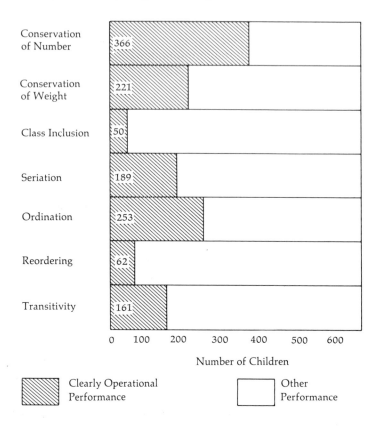

Number of Children

Clearly Operational Performance

Other Performance

Lovell studied the cognitive development of students in history. He concludes:

> In this kind of study it has repeatedly been shown that pupils' answers can be classified as preoperational, concrete operational, and formal operational, with other replies at intermediate points between these stages.
>
> At the level specified as concrete operational, answers clearly show: (1) ability to use the information provided but limited to what is immediately apparent in the text; (2) ability to forecast a result from the evidence but unable to form a mature hypothesis; and (3) movement from one point of view to another but no attempt to coordinate the two or more points of view. On the other hand, at the level specified as formal operational thought we do find evidence that the pupil goes beyond the given, tries out his thinking in a systematic manner, reasons by implication at an abstract level, attempts to relate different variables, and realizes a multiplicity of possible links. . . . However, our data do suggest that formal thought in history comes late; a mental age of 16 to 16½ years seems to be necessary. Studies at Leeds in other subject areas have likewise shown that pupils' answers can be assessed as being at the stages of preconcrete, or formal operational thought.[37]

---

[37] Lovell, "Some Problems . . . ," pp. 84–85. Used with permission of McGraw-Hill Book Co.

Many University Students Do Not Excel on Formal Tasks

Research done in Europe and the United States indicates that many college students do not do well on formalistic science and mathematical tasks.[38] Piaget suggests that his research determining the level of formal-operational thinking may have been based on a "privileged population," especially since studies done in Nancy, France, and New York did not agree with his results.[39]

Joe W. McKinnon and John W. Renner administered Piagetian tasks to 131 freshmen at Oklahoma City University. They found that 50 percent of the students operated completely at the concrete level and that another 25 percent had not fully attained the formal level. McKinnon further found that freshmen involved in inquiry-oriented science instruction at the university significantly improved in their formal ability on the tasks he administered.[40]

Why some university students do not do well on formal-operational tasks needs to be determined. As indicated by McKinnon and Renner, there clearly is much to be done to insure that graduates leave universities with well-developed cognitive minds.

Being Nonformalistic Sometimes a Hindrance

The realization by some students that they are not good thinkers (not formalistic) probably influences their choice of courses. For example, Ball and Sayre found only eleven physics students out of fifty-seven interviewed were not fully formalistic on the tasks administered.[41] Many students probably do not enroll in the course because they have heard that physics is difficult. It is interesting to note that enrollment in physics courses has been declining for a number of years. If this situation is to be changed, it seems reasonable that either a massive effort is needed to insure better operational achievement of students prior to the time they will take physics, or the instruction and evaluation in the course must not be based heavily on formalistic reasoning, e.g., being able to perform abstract mathematical operations. If this is done, students will be more likely to think they can be successful in the course. Although physics instruction might emphasize more concrete-operational learning situations, it should still retain as one of its main objectives helping students to attain formalistic patterns of thought. Much needs to be done to determine how this might be accomplished and to test whether these suggestions will help reduce the declining enrollments. Educators need also to look at other areas of the curriculum to see if this "I can't do it" syndrome is affecting the enrollments in other courses, particularly where logical-mathematical reasoning is required.

---

38 Ruth Beard, *An Outline of Piaget's Developmental Psychology for Students and Teachers* (New York: Basic Books, 1969), p. 113.

39 Jean Piaget, "Intellectual Evolution from Adolescence to Adulthood," (3rd International Convention and Awarding of Foneme Prizes, Foneme Institution for Studies and Research in Human Formation, Milan, Italy, May 9–10, 1970), pp. 160–65.

40 Joe W. McKinnon and John W. Renner, "Are Colleges Concerned with Intellectual Development," *American Journal of Psychology* 39 (September 1971): 1047–52.

41 Ball and Sayre, "Relationships between Student Piagetian...."

What Is Beyond the Formal?

Piaget states that he believes there well might be further mental development beyond the formal-operational level. He says of the period between ages fifteen and twenty: "The vital question that we feel must be answered is to discover whether, at this level of development as at previous levels, there exist cognitive structures common to all individuals. . . ."[42] Certainly, there is wide cognitive diversity among university students even though they may be formalistic. Research needs to clarify why some adults are better thinkers than others. Doing so will aid educators in designing better learning environments to effect greater self-actualization of all students.

Individualizing Instruction

As indicated by the work of Almy, Ball, Sayre, Elkind, McKinnon, and Renner, several studies have been done assessing a student's operational ability from the elementary school to the university.[43] All of these studies have shown there are students with various operational attainments in every class. In no classroom did all students perform well on all tasks administered to them, and the evidence indicates many students were at different Piagetian levels of development. To teach students as though they were all the same in large group instruction is certainly of questionable value. This is especially so if the function of the teacher is to try to develop logical-mathematical reasoning.

Teachers should evaluate students' cognitive abilities. If they cannot perform certain operations, they should be involved in activities contributing to the development of these abilities. Although activities to achieve this end have met with varied success, it seems reasonable that involving children in performing operational tasks approximating their ability level will better insure their attainment. With time and further research, it may well be possible to devise a series of activities to facilitate progressional achievement and even to help in making the transition from one stage to another. Clearly, Piaget's work and the research of other investigators indicate greater attention needs to be given to individualizing instruction to insure better cognitive development and operational sophistication.

There are many schools throughout this country making inroads into individualized instructional systems. Unfortunately, the organization of their curricular materials often does not strive to find out what the student knows prior to his involvement in the program, neither does it assess and diagnose operational difficulties. We need a concerted effort by teacher-training institutions to train teachers in Piagetian theory and individualizing instruction so that they may competently achieve this end. Endeavoring to modify instruction to this purpose requires a fundamentally different view of education than is presently held by many teachers. Often instructors see themselves as givers of information. A Piagetian-oriented teacher, however, is a facilitator—one who organizes the

---

[42] Jean Piaget, "Intellectual Evolution from Adolescence . . . ," p. 1964.

[43] For a summary of other related studies see Lovell, "Some Problems Associated . . . ," pp. 81–83.

instruction so that the individual is involved not only in learning information but also in using and developing the mind.

Although there is a necessity for individualizing instruction, there is still a need for group involvement. Remember, Piaget has pointed out the role of social interaction and its contribution to intelligence. Even though schools may individualize instruction, they must still give attention to designing student activities requiring social interaction, allowing students freedom of choice in learning activities, and allowing time to investigate in depth the material under study. If this is done, obviously there will need to be, particularly in the elementary school, an abdication of twenty- to thirty-minute blocks of time devoted to a subject area.

Correction of Perceptual Problems by Motor Training

Piaget believes that the basis of intellect is action. It is important for the child to have opportunities to act upon objects. Through such actions, children develop perceptual ability providing the basis for cognitive development.

Research indicates children may have nonphysiological perceptual problems causing learning disabilities. Some psychologists believe this may be due to a lack of physical experience during the sensory-motor period. Newell Kephart, in separate work from that of Piaget, has come to this conclusion. He has devised diagnostic remedial techniques for children suffering from these maladies. He suggests these children be given opportunities to use their bodies in sensory-motor ways. In a sense, he strives to have them reinact the sensory-motor period of their life.

Kephart, like Piaget, believes that first learning is essentially derived from sensory-motor experience and that this in turn influences later cognitive development. If a child has deficient or faulty experiences during this period of development, his mental ability is affected as a consequence. To rectify such inadequacies, Kephart initially involves children in performing various types of motor patterns: crawling, balancing the body, throwing, catching, manipulating and grasping objects, etc., until they become proficient in performing these. He then attempts to transfer this motor skill to perceptual ability so that they develop what he calls *perceptual-motor match*. This, he explains, is the process whereby the child increasingly uses his mind in the perceptual process to interact through muscular responses (motor reaction) with the environment. Motor explorations are the final arbitrators of all sensory information. Later in Kephart's progressional approach, he tries to develop what he calls *form perception* and *space structure*. He says:

> Normally, the child develops through these various stages during the pre-school years and by the age of six or seven has achieved a space structure. In many children, however, the developmental process has broken down; at one of the earlier stages, the child either failed to develop further or developed in an atypical or distorted manner. Such breakdowns in the de-developmental sequence may be the result of environmental deprivations, injuries or defects in the organism, or emotional pressures with which the child has been unable to cope. Many of these breakdowns reveal themselves in

the early elementary grades through difficulties in learning and low academic achievement.[44]

A teacher may be alerted to children's perceptual problems by observing
whether they have difficulty in identifying certain letters or words. The instructor
might test this further by having a child copy certain figures or letters. If the
student is unable to do this well, he should be given many experiences with
physical objects, for example, work with blocks placing them in boxes so that
they just fit, draw various shapes, form things with his hands from clay. The
child also may be given several figures and letters to trace until he does them
with ease. Drawing circles, such as most of us did in learning how to write, may
be particularly helpful to children having these problems.

After the child accomplishes these tasks with ease, he should be returned to
reading and writing. If he still has trouble, his problem may be due to some other
difficulty and be in need of specialized professional assistance. The clinical evidence supporting Kephart's theory is significant, but there is still need for further
research evidence.

Mental Health

For instruction to have an optimum influence on mental development, it must be
designed to fit the cognitive ability of the child. A curriculum too advanced may
force the student to rely on memorizing answers without understanding, in an
attempt to satisfy the teacher (in other words, little assimilation or accommodation). This type of situation can only have a crippling effect on the cognitive development of the child.

Parents and teachers knowledgeable of Piaget's work are less likely to cause
such mental scars. Piaget stresses the importance of adults accepting the cognitive
levels of children and loving them for their evolving mental growth. Unfortunately, the word *acceptance* has several diverse semantical interpretations in our
language, one of which really means not to accept, as indicated below:

1. I guess I have to accept that. This really means I do not accept it.
2. I accept and condone your actions.
3. I accept but do not necessarily condone your actions.

Too many parents and teachers think of acceptance as meaning condoning.
Because of this, they often react to children in negative ways when they cannot
condone their actions, causing children to build poor self-concepts.

An example of this was described by a twenty-six-year-old student in one of
my classes when we were discussing the process of reversibility. The student told
me that when he was six years old he would occasionally go from his small town
to a large city with his father. One day his father decided to play a game with him

---

[44] Newell C. Kephart, *The Slow Learner in the Classroom* (Columbus, Ohio: Charles E.
Merrill Publishing Co., 1960), p. 120.

requiring cognitive involvement. He asked his son to memorize the towns they passed through in order from their small community to the city. The child, surprisingly for his age, did do this, and the father was happy, as was the son because he made his father feel good. This was followed with several similar experiences each time they went to the city. One day, however, when they and some friends were returning from the city to their small town, the father wanted his son to give the names of the towns they passed through on the way home. The father did not realize he was requiring his son to name the towns in the reverse order, a task the child had not done and was, in fact, incapable of doing since it required reversible thinking. Reversible thought characterizes the concrete-operational child, and this child was in transition from the preoperational stage and could not yet perform this operation.

Not knowing this, the parent became very irate (nonaccepting) because his child could not demonstrate what his father thought was a relatively simple task. The child certainly was unable to comprehend why his father became irate because he couldn't reverse the order. However, he knew his father was mad at him and thought him stupid. The emotional trauma of this episode affected the child and still remains, as evidenced by his being able to relate it in detail some twenty years later. How many other ways did this parent negate his son's self-concept by being unaware of cognitive development?

Parents and teachers who try to apply Piaget's work, certainly are more likely to avoid such crippling cognitive episodes, particularly if they learn to accept humans in the sense that "I accept but I don't necessarily condone." For example, "I accept you as a preoperational child, but I don't condone your being preoperational for life."

Emotional Problems

Young children can sense rejection, love or lack of love, sincerity, etc., but they do not intellectualize about it as do more cognitively advanced individuals. For example, if you tell a child you like him, he probably will believe you and go around saying, "He likes me." An adolescent, on the other hand, may use his mind and ask, "Why is he saying that? Does he really like me or is he trying to get me to do something? (propositional thought) What's in it for him? Am I really likeable?"

Because the formalistic child has a relatively sophisticated mind, he is more likely to become concerned with "self" and, therefore, experience mental depression and elation. Parents and teachers need to be alerted to children's changes of mind because of their development and, as a result, adjust how they interact with children. It is reasonable when children become formalistic that adults should expect them to intellectualize about their emotions. For example, when a child expresses some disgust with some facet of his personality, the adult might say: "Supposing that what you say is true, how will you go about changing it?" By doing this, the adult indicates he respects the individual. By asking the question he implies the adolescent is capable of outlining a plan of action (making and doing hypothetical and propositional thought). Positively oriented responses assisting the child to use his formalistic faculties help to insure that the child uses these responses in positive rather than negative ways, thus contributing toward his maturity into adulthood.

Work and Its Cognitive Contributions

Adolescents demonstrate an intellectual egocentric idealism often contributing to emotional unrest. This arises from their newly developed rational abilities. As a result, they tend to center on what appears to be logical, negating what is real. They confuse their logically derived ideals with what exists in the real environment, not seeming to realize that the world and its people are not always rational. Such beliefs may cause psychological problems because these individuals have difficulty understanding the society in which they exist. As a result, they often tend during this period to be strong social critics.

Piaget believes this egocentric, formalistic phase begins to decrease when the individual becomes involved in the real world of employment. This is so because it takes the person away from "the dangers of formalism back into reality."[45]

This brings up the questions about the value of work for concrete- and transitional-operational children. How does, e.g., having a paper route affect this cognitive aspect of the child? It is my observation from counseling students with emotional problems in the secondary schools that, when they obtained a job, their mental health often improved. Similar effects also occurred when students became involved in extracurricular work such as: band, rally teams, glee club, plays, student government, and athletic events. Other psychologists, although coming to a similar conclusion through a different route, support Piaget's belief in the value of work and its mental contributions.[46]

Morals Evolve with Cognitive Stages

Clinical psychologists and psychiatrists have invested a considerable amount of their energies in studying Piaget's work because of the insights it gives into the operations of the normal child's mind. Of special interest to them is Piaget's study into the moral development of the individual.

As children develop, the way they look at what is good and bad also evolves. An infant may not be very cooperative in the early morning hours in allowing his parents to sleep. When the child is up, everybody should be up. The preoperational child, because of his egocentrism, tends to believe the way he looks at things is the only way they are. Because of this outlook, he may be exasperating in game playing since he does not accept rules other than his own.

The concrete-operational child, on the other hand, accepts the mandate of external rules. As a consequence, he begins to enjoy group games. However, he tends to believe that rules are externally fixed and unalterable. The idea that rules

---

[45] B. Inhelder and J. Piaget, *The Growth of Logical Thinking from Childhood to Adolescence*, trans. Anne Parsons and Stanley Pilgram (New York: Basic Books, 1958), p. 346.
[46] Abrahan H. Maslow, *The Farther Reaches of Human Experience* (New York: Viking Press, 1971).

can be agreed upon by consensus escapes him. Rules, like the directives he receives from his parents, are derived externally and are authoritarian in origin.

When a child begins to think in formal-operational terms, he is no longer content to accept external directives for his behavior from authoritarian figures. This is the period of adolescent rebellion or revolt from strong parental or institutional constrictions. Because the child is a hypothetical-deductive and propositional thinker, he can reason about what effect a change in rules will have on the playing of games or on his social interactions with other people. If parents or teachers fail to recognize this change in cognitive development and still act authoritatively, they are bound to engender conflict and a rebellious attitude in the adolescents under their care. During the formal-operational period, children may be given directives, but explanations for these are far more important so that the child can understand the reason for them. Children's thoughts should always be considered, but, during adolescence, it is of paramount importance.

A psychologist related to me an incident in which he respected the intellect of his own children. One night at dinner, as was his custom, he talked over family problems with his children and wife. He announced that the family's financial situation was fairly good and that they had several hundred dollars to spend. He asked them how they thought the money should be spent. An exciting discussion ensued in which all individual's ideas were given equal consideration. At the end of the dinner, the father suggested that they think the matter over further and later carry on their dialogue in order to better understand the desires of all members of the family. At the end of the week, the discussion narrowed to the purchase of either a color television set or a piano. The two young teen-agers of the family gave arguments for the purchase of a piano. The family purchased the piano. These parents realized the importance of not only respecting the values of their children but also of giving them opportunities to learn how to establish values. This is very important, particularly during the formal-operational period and beyond. It is difficult to conceive of these children rebelling against parental authority because the authority was really democratic. It even seems more inconceivable that these children will feel the necessity of, for example, running away from home, becoming hooked on drugs, or committing suicide in an attempt to establish self-identity. The awareness by teachers and parents of moral development and the need for children to evolve value systems should help lessen these ills. Piaget has shown the need and importance of equilibration. Children must have the right to derive and accommodate their own value structures. To do any less will lead to a deprivation of the individual and contribute to poor mental health. More is said on ethical development in Chapter 9.

Application of Piaget's Theory Must Be Made with Caution

One danger with the introduction of any new psychological theory is that its originator may be considered an oracle. Piaget is no oracle; he is only a man, but a man who has given us almost fifty years of research into the cognitive development of the child. Much of what Piaget says is disputed by psychologists. This is particularly true in respect to his model of why the mind behaves in the manner it does. Does it assimilate, accommodate, equilibrate? Are there really stages?

His theory is an extrapolation from his research data. The inferences he makes, such as those of equilibration and stages, are open to question. Among some developmental psychologists, there is agreement that the stages of development do exist and that they follow a sequence. There is a wealth of replication studies to support these stages, although some psychologists are not convinced of this fact.[47] Because of the results of some studies, Piaget now believes that the age span for the periods he has defined is only an approximation and may vary considerably from one environment to another. He maintains, however, that it has been supported by many research studies that individuals progress through stages in sequence. There is no jumping of periods, for example, from the preoperational to the formal operational. Piaget says in this respect:

> Each stage is necessary for the following one. If this were not the case, one would be in no position to talk of stages. Naturally, the ages at which different children reach the stages may vary. In some social environments the stages are accelerated, whereas in others they are more or less systematically retarded. This differential development shows that stages are not purely a question of the maturation of the nervous system but are dependent upon interaction with the social environment and with experience in general. The order, however, remains constant.[48]

However, a word of caution should be mentioned in using the concept of stage. Stage defines the general characteristics of a group of individuals during a period of their lives. An interviewer, when talking to a particular child, may determine that he conserves and thereby infer that this cognitive ability generalizes to all tasks. It seems reasonable that if a child has a cognitive structure he should be able to use this rational ability in solving related problems. However, such has not been proven to be the case. For example, a child may conserve mass before he conserves volume. He may, furthermore, indicate the attainment of some operational ability through his actions but demonstrate a lag (this lag is referred to by Piaget as a *décalage*) on the verbal level.

For this reason, one should use great discretion in classifying children on an operational level based upon the administration of a few Piagetian tasks. All that you can really say, for example, is that the child was concrete operational on four of the tasks and formal on two, then formulate other items to further test his cognitive level. A teacher or parent in interacting with a child in a logical-mathematical manner should assume the role of an interviewer in determining the operational ability of the child so as to better communicate with him. To formulate questions, give tasks, and ask the child to justify his answers takes

---

[47] J. H. Flavell, *The Developmental Psychology of Jean Piaget* (New York: D. Van Nostrand Co., 1963), pp. 357–402. See also L. Abate, "Frequency of Citation Study in Child Psychology Literature," *Child Development* 40 (1968): 87–92.

[48] Jean Piaget, "The Theory of Stages in Cognitive Development," in *Measurement and Piaget, . . .*, p. 7. Used with permission of McGraw-Hill Book Co.

considerable sophistication and learning by the adult. The effort, however, leads to greater cognitive wisdom insuring interacting more effectively with the child.

Since Piaget's theory is still in a state of modification and in need of verification by investigators, it should be used with discretion. The real test of the value of his theory is how it helps individuals to better work with children—to understand them, aid in the manifestation of all their human talents, accept them as persons *becoming*, facilitate their cognitive growth, and fathom their epistemological development.

Suggestions
for
Teaching 8

The following pages, in addition to those ideas outlined in Chapter 7, are specific suggestions for instruction based on Piaget's theory. This outline is by no means exhaustive but should act as a springboard to assist individuals in making the translation of the theory into practice. As you become more aware of Piaget's work and how to apply it, many other ideas will undoubtedly manifest themselves and stimulate your utilization of the cognitive-developmental viewpoint.

Above all, as you read these suggestions, keep in mind Piaget has shown that development and manifestation of potential are basic to human life. As teachers it is essential that we expand both our own and our students' growth so that there is a movement toward greater awareness, higher levels of consciousness, and discovery of one's being. It is the nature of our species to grow or die; as such, we must help others to ascend toward increased mental growth and fulfillment or else we negate our humanness.

I. *When you work with children, remember the main concepts of cognitive development.*

1. Children develop cognitively, passing through four main stages of mental development during maturation.

2. Children of the same chronological age may vary considerably in the understanding and performance of mental operations.

3. Just because a child may perform a task that is formal-operational, does not necessarily indicate she is formal. That is, many tasks must be given to an individual in order to determine cognitive level.

4. The development of a person's cognitive ability is of real relevance to that individual.

5. There are two main types of experiences: physical (learning information), and logical-mathematical (learning to perform mental opera-

tions). Physical experience occurs when children physically act on objects in the environment. They begin to realize that action is complex; for example, they find that objects may be ordered from short to long or vice versa. From physical experiences, the child becomes initiated into logical-mathematical experiences. Eventually the child learns mental structures which she will use to grasp abstract concepts.

6. A student only learns to reason by having experiences that allow or stimulate thinking.

II. *An educational environment fosters the development of a person's ethical level.*

As a person evolves cognitively, she also progresses to higher stages of ethical development; however, it is only with education that this parallel development occurs.

III. *Design activities to involve students in social interaction.*

Children decrease in egocentricity through active social interaction because they are confronted with different views. They begin to find that the way they understand life is not the only viewpoint. Interaction involving argument and critical analysis is the raw material for developing higher cognitive abilities.

IV. *An understanding of cognitive level will enable you to determine readiness for certain tasks.*

A student must have the abilities gained in the appropriate level before she may deal successfully with the required task.

V. *Avoid pseudo-learning.*

Pseudo-learning occurs when students neither assimilate nor accommodate information. In such a case, children are required to memorize (an equation, for example) without understanding or are presented material beyond their cognitive level.

VI. *Form an operational curriculum.*

1. Stress intellectual development. It is not enough to teach just for facts; you must help students reach their human potential. Piaget's efforts have made intellectual development an important facet of a curriculum. This has particularly influenced curriculum innovators and teachers at preschools and elementary schools to perceive children in a global, humane way rather than just as assimilators of the three Rs.

2. Follow Piaget's sequence of development in your curriculum. Since children pass through a sequence of growth stages, the curriculum must be designed appropriately.

3. Adapt to where the child is developmentally. Construct the curriculum to deal with the child's needs; do not wait until the child has met your criteria for entrance to the curriculum.

4. Utilize the "moderately novel" principle. Piaget believes that presenting children with moderately novel problems only slightly above their cognitive level assists them in advancing to higher degrees of operational ability. Let students choose their own problem-oriented tasks; they will usually choose things that are challenging.

5. Use Piaget's theory in any culture. Since Piagetian levels are universal, they provide a predictive base for constructing curriculum materials for any culture and country. Recall, however, that foreign, minority, and lower socio-economical cultures may vary in the rate they progress through growth stages.

6. Stress learning through action- and discovery-oriented activities. Students learn only when they act mentally on what is being investigated. Curriculum materials should be oriented toward discovery, inquiry, and creativity to help students work mentally. Provide activities for the student to make decisions and verify and deduce conclusions. Laboratory and field experiences should require students to use thinking processes such as hypothesizing, inferring, designing experiments, and formulating models.

7. Involve students physically and mentally. Students should be involved both physically and mentally in acting on what is being learned. Rather than having them always listen, have them read or create something and then share in small groups their views about the project's important qualities, creative value, and possible further activities. The groups then should decide what conclusions they wish to report to the class for discussion and evaluation.

8. Create more interaction; allow small groups to work on problems. Students resolving a problem in small groups of three to five facilitates more learning than do class discussions due to greater student involvement and the advantage of a mix of individuals at different cognitive levels. Cognitively advanced students model for the less developed persons.

9. Involve students in role playing. Have them play roles in resolving problems. For example, students may take the part of famous scientists or public officials. This activity provides opportunities to perceive different viewpoints (thus reducing egocentricity), and involves active participation in the studied subject.

10. Use value clarification and conflict strategies. Value-oriented activities within small groups give students opportunities to develop their cognitive processes. The students must resolve value conflicts within the group by perceiving viewpoints other than their own. In turn, open-mindedness fosters more viable alternatives in their thinking.

11. Move from the concrete to the abstract. Educational materials and class activities should preferably start with the concrete and progress to an abstract level rather than the reverse.

12. Do not always use the direct approach. Research indicates that the direct way of attacking a problem, such as language development, may not always be the best way. For example, investigations by McAfee at the preschool of the University of Northern Colorado indicate that sorting objects facilitated the development of language in children, particularly those of Spanish American origin. Bruner also found that young children who play with available materials acquire just as much education as those who learn in structured class situations.

VII. *Attempt to develop personal qualities of a good teacher.*

1. Ask more questions than you give answers, especially divergent questions. Students should get involved in finding out and analyzing the meaning of what is being learned. Questions allowing for divergent answers stimulate creative and critical thinking. Convergent questions answered by *yes* or *no* should be avoided. When children make contradictions, say, "But you said a little while ago that . . . " or "Which do you mean?"

2. Talk less and listen more, stressing nonverbal instruction. Sense when to be quiet. After asking a question wait several seconds, at least five, for their answers. Remember, children need time to assimilate and accommodate information before they can respond intelligently. Concern yourself with the development of the individual rather than with how much of the subject the student covers (be student centered, not subject centered).

3. Allow freedom of choice. Encourage and give students freedom to choose some of their learning activities so that they may use their minds to evaluate what should be studied. In this manner, they learn to develop commitment toward their studies.

4. Do not correct a pupil's error in reasoning. Rather, ask questions and provide experiences so that she can correct her own mistakes.

5. Determine cognitive levels by giving them conservation or formal reasoning tasks and by asking questions to determine how they think. For example, if you wish to assess the formal level you may ask them to perform reflexive thinking processes. In science and math you might desire the student to describe her mental steps toward resolving a problem. If your students do not perform well on problems of this nature, they have not yet achieved the formal stage.

6. Learn to accept the fact that students may mature cognitively at different rates. Individuals who are behind their peers now may be equally capable in adulthood. Be aware also that most classes will have students at more than one level, in addition to many in transitional stages.

VIII. *Specific suggestions for the Preoperational Level, four to seven years.*

1. Make sure that children manipulate and group objects.

2. Involve preschool children in activities requiring social interaction so that they may reduce their egocentricity.

3. Encourage children in play such as "house," and "store," where they can act out various roles.

4. Ask children to make comparisons. Create activities where children need to know "which is," for example, which is taller, bigger, wider, heavier, or longer.

5. Place a few bottle caps in two rows varying in length. Everyone should count and compare the rows. Ask students to connect one row of bottle caps to the other by placing straws on the caps which run parallel in each row. Have pupils count the number in each row. This type of activity may have to be repeated many times with different objects before children will conserve number.

6. Encourage children to line up in rows from tall to short and vice versa so that they may become more involved in ordering operations. Give children tasks where they have opportunities to order objects.

7. Have pupils weigh objects. Let them play with balances and teeter-totter-like toys.

8. Bring in various examples of life cycles of animals and plants such as several pictures of butterfly development or the sprouting of bean and corn seeds. Examples of natural stages help children develop ordering ability.

9. Have children draw scenes with perspective. Encourage them to draw objects in approximately the same location as they are viewed; for example, if they see a cow in the far end of a field they should place the cow similarly on the paper. They should also try to copy geometrical figures, some open and unconnected (like a half circle) others connected (like a square). Give them some outlines within which they would have to include objects or exclude objects; for example, they can be instructed to draw a square with a circle inside it, an ellipse with an arrow drawn tangent to it, or a few triangles with small circles inside and surrounding.

10. Have children tilt a closed container with colored liquid and draw how the water inside appears with the container slanted, upright, or laying flat. This activity may be repeated using several different types of plastic or glass containers such as those emptied of pop or milk.

11. Construct an inclined plain or hill. Place together different size marbles on top of it and let the children roll these down the hill and compare how they finish. This should help children eventually gain a concept of speed.

12. Ask children to justify their answers when making logical-mathematical types of conclusions. For example, when they say that a

liquid poured from a tall glass into several glasses will still contain the same volume of liquid, ask, "Why do you think so? How would you prove that to another student?"

IX. *Specific Suggestions for the Concrete-Operational Level, seven to eleven years.*

1. Continue any preoperational activities you believe are relevant for children in this age group such as conservation tasks.

2. Encourage children to discover concepts and principles. Although you should refrain from telling them outright, you may formulate questions relevant to what is being studied in order to help them focus on some aspect of their learning. Remember, it is necessary for children to assimilate and accommodate on their own.

3. Involve children in operational tasks such as adding, subtracting, multiplying, dividing, ordering, seriating, reversing, etc., preferably in concrete ways where they utilize objects. Later you may introduce mathematical symbols.

4. Plan activities where students must grasp the idea of an ascending and and descending classification hierarchy. Have them place the following in order: city of Denver, county of Denver, state of Colorado, United States, Western Hemisphere; or ducklings, ducks, birds, animals, organisms, etc.

5. Design many activities having children order and reverse order. Many third graders have problems in reversing order such as going from tall to short rather than from short to tall, or listing the cities they would pass through in taking a trip to a large metropolitan center and then reversing their order in coming home.

6. Involve students in using horizontal and vertical coordinates. Achieve this task by asking them to locate places on the city and state maps.

7. Present problems requiring students to isolate variables. Usually you will need to help students because they will not suggest all the possible variables.

8. In the advanced part of this stage have students construct theoretical models tied to concrete examples; for example, they may explain molecular theory through the use of concrete models of atoms rather than by symbols.

9. Include activities which require conservation of area, understanding of continuous quantity, weight, and displacement of volume.

10. Have children define and state problems.

11. Involve students in testing all possibilities toward resolving problems. Help them discover what strategies they use to solve problems.

12. Particularly continue to ask students to justify their answers to logical-mathematical problems and situations encountered in conservation tasks. Help students check the validity and accuracy of their conclusions.

X. *Specific suggestions for the Formal-Operational Level, eleven years and older.*

Students who are in transition to formal operations should be encouraged to perform formal reasoning. Seven operations developed at the formal level follow, with suggestions for activities, hypothetical situations, and dialogues given for illustrative purposes.

Hypothetical-Deductive Thinking

Situation

The teacher proposes a problem and invites students to make hypotheses.

Each student selects the hypothesis she feels is best, and then discards or rejects the others on the basis of a personal strategy of deduction.

Dialogue

TEACHER: "Imagine that there is a large rock weighing 300 pounds which must be moved. How would you move it?"

STUDENT 1: "It could be moved by using a chain hoist or block and tackle."

STUDENT 2: "It could be moved by prying it up with a plank and then putting logs under it to roll it on."

STUDENT 3: "It could be pulled up a plank onto a trailer with a winch."

STUDENT 4: "Using a plank as a lever and logs to roll it on would be the cheaper way, so I think that is the best way to do it."

Propositional Thinking

Situation

The teacher proposes a problem involving several factors. All, some, or none of these factors may be involved.

Dialogue

TEACHER: "A car ran into a ditch on a deserted road one night. The weather bureau stated that there had been scattered rain during the hours preceding the accident. Also an empty beer can was found in the wrecked car. What kinds of evidence might help to determine the cause of the accident? For example, how would you obtain evidence as to whether the road were wet when the accident occurred and if this were an important factor?"

STUDENT 1: "If it rained and the car was driven on dirt roads, then mud would collect on the undersides of the fenders. Mud might even collect if it had not rained, though."

STUDENT 2: "Or it might have collected at an earlier date."

STUDENT 3: "If it had then there would be no mud under the car."

STUDENT 4: "Even if there were a little rain, there still might not be any mud."

Evaluating Information

Situation	*Dialogue*
The teacher presents a problem and suggests several ways it might be approached. She then asks questions causing the students to evaluate using value schemes.	TEACHER: "Here are several ways to investigate robberies: . . . Which do you think is the best means and why do you think so? What things are good about each procedure? Which investigative method seems least likely to solve the problem?"
Students establish criteria in their minds and analyze each approach in terms of their personal criteria.	STUDENT 1: "Alternative 3 offers better controls over the variables involved."
	STUDENT 2: "The simplicity of the second approach and its low cost makes it more appealing."

Originating Problems

Situation	*Dialogue*
The teacher selects a topic familiar to the class and asks questions related to it. The students have sufficient background to formulate problems.	TEACHER: "What influential factors should we consider if we were trying to bring the economy into better balance? (Other problems which could be discussed include conserving natural resources, eliminating diseases such as cancer, improving nutrition for the poor, and protecting the beauty of our land from pollution.)
	STUDENT 1: "The gross national product and income per capita."
	STUDENT 2: "Interest rates, stock market levels, and the number of new housing areas."
	TEACHER: "Which of these do you think is the biggest problem?"
	STUDENT 3: "Interest levels."

STUDENT 4: "Some other important problems are the government controls imposed by the Federal Reserve Board and the legislative hurdles involved in making changes."

TEACHER: "Which problems should we study?"

Reflexive Thinking

Situation

The teacher asks the students to discuss a problem in such a way that they will reflect on their prior conclusions.

Dialogue

TEACHER: "What steps did you go through in solving this problem?"

STUDENT 1: "I considered the variables involved and then selected those which could be controlled easily and those that could not be. Next, I devised an experiment to find out what happens."

TEACHER: "If you were going to do this experiment again, how would you get better data?"

STUDENT 2: "It would have been better if I had made measurements more frequently."

TEACHER: "If you were going to re-write your report, what things would you change?"

STUDENT 3: "I would organize it around my major findings rather than chronologically."

TEACHER: "What is the nature of the problem? What things were known, and what things were unknown? What steps did you follow in solving it?"

Theoretical and Ethical Thinking

Formal-operational students are capable of determining and synthesizing general properties, theories, values, and ethics. Therefore, they should be given many opportunities to discuss ethical questions and devise and discover general laws and theories in science, history, philosophy, and mathematics. Some projects such as the McREL Inquiry Role (Mid Continent Regional Educational Laboratory) and others have incorporated these experiences into their curricula. The course materials in such projects enable concrete-operational students to observe their classmates' reasoning and model formal thinking. Many value-clarification strategies used in social studies and sciences are also used in this manner.

Thinking in Areas of Interest and Good Background

Students should be encouraged especially to think formally in areas where they have interest and background because personal interest in a topic helps to elevate thinking levels and to increase involvement in learning activities. Let them decide for themselves the best ways to organize steps in completing a task. Make arrangements for students to work together in small groups, especially if you know that one student is relatively formal and others are more transitional. Motivate students to collaborate in any task with their peers. Interact with students while they work on investigations and ask them how they are going about collecting and interpreting their data. Ask them to derive conclusions about ethical and moral questions. Remember, above all, the greater the student involvement in resolving problems both individually and through social interaction, the greater the learning and chances for formal development.

> **Now go to MEDIAPAK E. When you have completed it, return to this text and take the Self-evaluation Inventory for Chapters 7 and 8 and MEDIAPAK E.**

Self-evaluation Inventory

Directions: Listed below are some of the main topics covered in Chapters 7 and 8 and MEDIAPAK E. Read each statement and rate it on the scale TWICE: once according to what you knew about the topic before starting this part of the program and again according to what you have learned after completing it. Circle the appropriate number and mark B for before and A for after next to it, as indicated below.

Topic	*Student Evaluation*					
	Low		*Moderate*		*High*	
Example: Important Piagetian mental operations.	1	②B 3		4	⑤A	6
1. Evocational memory	1	2	3	4	5	6
2. Recognitional memory	1	2	3	4	5	6
3. Reconstructive memory	1	2	3	4	5	6
4. The correlation of memory with development	1	2	3	4	5	6
5. The role of cognitive experience	1	2	3	4	5	6
6. How Piaget's theory can be used to determine readiness	1	2	3	4	5	6
7. The role of social interaction in cognitive development	1	2	3	4	5	6
8. How to avoid pseudo-learning	1	2	3	4	5	6
9. Designing a curriculum	1	2	3	4	5	6

10. Utilizing the "moderately novel" principle   1   2   3   4   5   6

11. International significance of Piaget's theory   1   2   3   4   5   6

12. Action as basic to learning   1   2   3   4   5   6

13. Not all children attain the highest levels of cognitive development   1   2   3   4   5   6

14. Need to be more of a questioner than an answerer   1   2   3   4   5   6

15. Need to talk less and involve students more   1   2   3   4   5   6

16. Need to listen and react to children on their cognitive level   1   2   3   4   5   6

17. Need to allow freedom of choice in selecting some areas of study   1   2   3   4   5   6

18. The importance of not demeaning a student because she is not cognitively as mature as others of the same age   1   2   3   4   5   6

19. The importance of not preventing students from taking a class because of lack of cognitive advancement. (For example, physics teachers often discriminate against the concrete-operational students.)   1   2   3   4   5   6

20. The realization a class contains at least three different cognitive level clusters   1   2   3   4   5   6

21. The importance of confronting children with their contradictions   1   2   3   4   5   6

22. The need to stress hands-on and total body involvement   1   2   3   4   5   6

23. The importance of helping children through questioning to check the validity and accuracy of their conclusions   1   2   3   4   5   6

24. The importance of involving children in areas of interest and good background for cognitive development   1   2   3   4   5   6

25. The fact that cognitive investment in the young child pays off   1   2   3   4   5   6

26. The realization that early computation and reading tasks may be ineffective   1   2   3   4   5   6

27. The diagnostic value of Piagetian tests   1   2   3   4   5   6

28. The importance of small-group involvement in learning	1	2	3	4	5	6
29. The role of the discovery approach in learning	1	2	3	4	5	6
30. The necessity of proper timing so that children have time to assimilate and accommodate	1	2	3	4	5	6
31. The realization that both physical and mental experiences are important	1	2	3	4	5	6
32. A child's mind is not an adult mind	1	2	3	4	5	6
33. The realization that because a child cannot fully understand a situation does not mean she should not be physically involved in it, for example, teeter-tottering	1	2	3	4	5	6
34. Realization that preschool children do not understand admonishments involving reasoning	1	2	3	4	5	6
35. Need to question more and answer less	1	2	3	4	5	6
36. The advantages of students being involved in role playing	1	2	3	4	5	6
37. The cognitive role of value clarification activities	1	2	3	4	5	6
38. The importance of being patient in trying to understand the logic of the child	1	2	3	4	5	6

Now that you have assessed your growth after reading Chapters 7 and 8 and completing MEDIAPAK E, review those areas above where you indicate lack of growth or confidence about the topic. Then continue with Chapter 9.

Piaget's and Kohlberg's Theories of Moral Development 9

Since moral development is so much a part of becoming a fully functioning individual, a special consideration of this topic is included here. This information, furthermore, represents how Piagetian theory is being used as a springboard for further research and how it is being applied to the educational process.[1]

An holistic and humanistic approach to education should be devoted to aiding the individual manifest his total potential. As a person develops, he acquires morals, attitudes, and values influencing learning. For adults to ignore this part of development is to lessen their educational effectiveness in interacting with children. Educators have long been concerned with including values and morals as an integral part of the educational process. John Dewey, for example, pointed out the futility of not attending to values, since students during the schooling years are simultaneously developing them and are influenced by the learning environment in their attainment.

Piaget's Stages of Moral Development

Piaget's research has substantiated Dewey's thesis by revealing the developmental character of value achievement in the maturation process, particularly during the school years. Piaget found that children's views of the world and ethics passed through various stages:

1. Egocentric:
   (0-4 years)

   A child during this period believes the way he sees things is the way they are for everybody. He is unable to play a game since his rules are *the* rules. He can not perceive how another person could have different rules.

2. Authoritarian:
   (4-11 years)

   Rules and ethics come from authority figures.

---

[1] Much of Piaget's research has been devoted to the subject of moral development; see Piaget, *The Moral Development of the Child* (New York: The Free Press, 1969).

3. Consensus Derived: Rules or ethics may be arrived at by consensus as to what is
   (11 plus years)   good, etc. This is the beginning of self-evaluation of values
                         which may continue into full adulthood.

Although the above outline of Piaget's research is somewhat simplified, it conveys sufficient information for educators to understand the essence of this developmental aspect of the individual.

Kohlberg's Ethical Stages

Lawrence Kohlberg, impressed by Piaget's research on moral development, used it as the foundation for advancing further investigation into this area. Kohlberg carried on numerous studies in this and other countries striving to better define the hierarchical progression of ethics as children pass through the maturation process. One of his main works involves a longitudinal study of boys starting at ages ten and sixteen and following their value evolvement past the ages of twenty-four and thirty. Kohlberg has also made several cross-cultural investigations in various parts of the world.

This research has further substantiated Piaget's belief that ethical attainment is hierarchical in character. Kohlberg believes it consists of three levels each containing stages (six in all) having a total of twenty-five different aspects.[2] The three levels are (1) preconventional or premoral, (2) conventional or conforming, and (3) post-conventional or self-accepting moral principles. A brief summary of these levels is outlined below.

Preconventional Level

At this level the child is responsive to such rules and labels as good and bad and right and wrong. He interprets these labels in purely physical or hedonistic terms: if he is bad, he is punished; if he is good, he is rewarded. He also interprets the labels in terms of the physical power of those who enunciate them—parents, teachers, and other adults. The level comprises the following two stages.

Stage 1: Punishment and Obedience Orientation. The physical consequences of action determine its goodness or badness regardless of the human meaning or value of these consequences. Avoidance of punishment and unquestioning deference to power are valued in their own right, not in terms of respect for an underlying moral order supported by punishment and authority, the latter being stage 4.

Stage 2: Instrumental Relativist Orientation. Right action consists of that which instrumentally satisfies one's own needs and occasionally the needs of others. Human relations are viewed in terms similar to those of the marketplace. Elements of fairness, reciprocity, and equal sharing are present, but they are always interpreted in a pragmatic way. Reciprocity is a matter of "you scratch my back and I'll scratch yours," not of loyalty, gratitude, or justice.

---

[2] Lawrence Kohlberg, "From Is to Ought: How to Commit the Naturalistic Fallacy and Get Away with It in the Study of Moral Development," in *Cognitive Development and Epistemology*, ed. T. Mischel (New York: Academic Press, 1971), p. 164.

Conventional Level

At this level the expectations of the individual's family, group, or nation is perceived as valuable in its own right, regardless of immediate and obvious consequences. The attitude is one not only of conformity to the social order but of loyalty to it; of actively maintaining, supporting, and justifying the order; and of identifying with the persons or group involved in it. This level comprises the following two stages.

Stage 3: Interpersonal Concordance or "Good Boy-Nice Girl" Orientation. Good behavior is that which pleases or helps others and is approved by them. There is much conformity to stereotypical images of what is majority or "natural" behavior. Behavior is frequently judged by intention. "He means well" becomes important, and one earns approval by being nice.

Stage 4: "Law and Order" Orientation. Authority, fixed rules, and the maintenance of the social order are valued. Right behavior consists of doing one's duty, showing respect for authority, and maintaining the social order for its own sake.

Postconventional Level

At this level there is a clear effort to teach a personal definition of moral values—to define principles that have validity and application apart from the authority of groups or persons and apart from the individual's own identification with these groups. Again, this level has two stages.

Stage 5: Social-Contract Legalistic Orientation. Generally, this stage has utilitarian overtones. Right action tends to be defined in terms of general individual rights and in terms of standards that have been critically examined and agreed upon by the whole society. There is a clear awareness of the importance of personal values and opinions and a corresponding emphasis on procedural rules for reaching consensus. Other than that which is constitutionally and democratically agreed upon, right is a matter of personal values and opinion. The result is an emphasis both upon the legal point of view and upon the possibility of making rational and socially desirable changes in the law, rather than freezing it as in the law and order stage 4. Outside the legal realm, free agreement is the binding element of obligation. This is the official morality of the U.S. government and the Constitution.

Stage 6: Universal Ethical-Principle Orientation. Right is defined by the conscience in accord with self-chosen principles, which in turn are based on logical comprehensiveness, universality, and consistency. These principles are abstract and ethical (the golden rule, the categorical imperative). They are not concrete moral rules like the Ten Commandments. At heart, these are universal principles of justice, of the reciprocity and equality of human rights, and of respect for the dignity of human beings as individual persons. These six stages are summarized below to capsulize the main aspects of Kohlberg's levels so as to better assist educators in their use.

Kohlberg's Levels of Moral Development

STAGES	MOTIVATION
Stage 1: Avoidance of Punishment	Wanting to avoid punishment. Self-gratification. Is moral mainly because of fear of punishment.
Stage 2: Prudence	Desire for reward and benefit. What is in it for me? What are the consequences?
Stage 3: Fear of Disapproval	Anticipation of disapproval or self-guilt. Has lots of stereotypes of nice and mean people.
Stage 4: Conformity to Authority	Anticipation of dishonor. Afraid of losing face or gaining dishonor. Follows social rules and rule maintaining. You can not make exceptions because everyone would start to do it.
Stage 5: Democratic or Legalistic Attitudes	Concern about self-respect or being irrational and inconsistent. Right actions—constitutional and democratically derived. Free agreement and contract is binding between individuals. It is the way the American government operates. Believes in equality of opportunity and civil law.
Stage 6: Universal Value for Life	Concern about condemnation, about violating a person's principles, and about maintaining principles as a way of life. Sacredness of life; compassion for fellow man, universal principle of justice.

As with Piaget, Kohlberg's levels are both hierarchical and invariant. This means that as individuals evolve they progress toward higher levels of development. They pass from an egocentric orientation of "what is in it for me" in stages 1 and 2, eventually to "compassion for mankind" in stage 6. The sequence of stages does not vary. An individual never skips a level. Furthermore, Kohlberg's theory, like Piaget's, is developmental because:

1. There is an invariant order of stages.
2. There exists hierarchical integration: the higher stages include the lower ones.
3. There is a progression to higher structured wholes because each level includes a new set of logical operations.

Children Do Not Always Behave at One Stage

Individuals do not typically respond in all situations on one stage. About 50 percent of the time, they will behave at a certain level which is considered their ethical stage. It should also be pointed out that all individuals may cheat at some time. However, those holding higher ethical principles are less likely to do so than their less principled peers. It is important, therefore, in assessing an individual's breach of ethics, to determine how principled they are since such incidents may in fact be rare. Corrective procedures should take this in mind and be administered accordingly.

Universality of Stages

Kohlberg has found that, although certain virtues and morals may vary from culture to culture, his moral stages are universal. Studies carried out with the Tayals (in Malaysia), Taiwanese, Mayas (in Mexico) Israelis, and Turks all confirmed this fact. There are, however, percentage differences among cultures as to the number found in each stage. For example, the number of sixteen year olds at stage 5 in the United States was significantly higher than in Mexico and Taiwan.[3]

Kohlberg also found that middle class children tend to be at a more advanced level than those from the lower classes. Since the percentage of middle class individuals varies with the country so does the number attaining these stages. Preliterate and semiliterate societies had an absence of people at stages 5 and 6.[4] Comparisons of individuals from Catholic, Protestant, Jewish, Buddhist, Moslem, and atheist backgrounds indicated no difference in the number reaching the higher ethical levels.

Correlation with Levels of Cognitive Ability

Kohlberg believes individuals pass from one ethical stage to another for the same reason that they progress cognitively, that is, through adapting and accommodating to the environment. Kohlberg believes that the development of ethical levels is dependent on the attainment of Piagetian stages because each new level of morality requires a set of logical operations not present in the prior stage.[5] Evidence for this conclusion comes from his research in which he found that 93 percent of children age five through seven capable of thinking on the concrete-operational level were able to do reversible operations at stage 2 of moral development, while those not able to think concretely were in stage 1 of moral development. On the other hand, few children who were on moral stages 3 or 4 failed to be able to perform inversion of reciprocity Piagetian tasks. Kohlberg found further that of all adolescents attaining stages 5 and 6 of ethical development, about 16 percent of the population were also formal thinkers. This is not to say, however, that formal thinkers will necessarily be at the higher levels of ethics. Kohlberg believes that the advantages of reasoning on one highest level may be evident to the individual, but the advantages of having high ethics may be less clear. Kohlberg also believes it is easier to think formally when considering physical entities, for example, the effects of gravitation, than it is to reason about moral issues. Research done by Kohlberg and others, indicates, further-

---

[3] Kohlberg, "From Is to Ought . . . ," p. 173.
[4] Kohlberg, "From Is to Ought . . . ," p. 174, 178.
[5] Kohlberg, "From Is to Ought . . . ," p. 186.

more, that moral maturity correlates positively with IQ but not as well as ability to solve Piagetian tasks.

Environmental Influence

The home environment contributes significantly to children's ethical development. Kohlberg found that children from higher socio-economic levels are more ethically advanced than children from lower levels. He believes this is essentially due to the difference in opportunities for children to assume roles of responsibility and in the difference of encouragement in participation in family discussions related to moral conflict situations. He further found that children popular in school progress to higher levels of development significantly faster than those who are unchosen by their peers. Presumably, it is the experience of taking roles in the homes that makes it possible for some children (participants) to advance over others (nonparticipants).

The importance of the environment is further reflected in studies done in orphanages and reform schools. Children raised in orphanages are mainly at the preconventional level, stages 1 and 2, even up to age sixteen. Children in reform schools are similarly low ethical achievers, being mainly at stage 2. However, research on the home, orphanages, and reform schools does not indicate that these environments necessarily have to include a warm and loving family for moral development to occur. Furthermore, Kohlberg found that Kibbutz youngsters in Israel achieved morally as well as middle class children in other cultures.[6]

For value attainment to occur there must be *just environment* in the home, school, and other institutions because it is through such surroundings that individuals gain opportunities to grow morally. For example, when students are confronted in class with situations interfering with learning, they should be asked what might be done to rectify the problems instead of the teacher's using authority to correct them. *Students cannot be expected to learn to interact with others humanely or to resolve value conflicts unless they have opportunities to do so and are treated justly.*

The necessity for a just environment presents a dilemma to many of our institutions. Reform schools and prisons largely interact with their wards on Kohlberg's first level—punishment. However, when individuals are returned to society, they must operate at higher levels. It is apparent, therefore, that part of the energy in reforming our social institutions should be devoted to providing opportunities for individuals to progress to higher ethical levels. To do otherwise is to perpetuate their present inadequacies.

Schools Contribute to Ethical Development

Research indicates that moral development can be positively influenced in school. Simon, Howe, and Kirschenbaum state that students exposed to value classifica-

---

[6] Kohlberg, "From Is to Ought . . . ," p. 191. See also M. Bar-yam and L. Kohlberg, "Development of Moral Judgment in the Kibbutz," in *Recent Research in Moral Development*, eds. L. Kohlberg and E. Turiel (New York: Holt Rinehart & Winston, 1971).

tion processes in the school are "less apathetic, have become less flighty, less conforming as well as less dissenting. They are more zestful, energetic, more critical in their thinking and are more likely to follow through on decisions. In the case of under-achievers, value clarification has led to better success in school."[7]

The purpose of value clarification is to aid students in developing processes to use in determining their own values. *It is not to indoctrinate.* An instructor must be open and accepting of students' views, helping them clarify their values. The teacher, furthermore, must insure that this attitude also prevails among the students for their classmates. In order to do this, Simon believes instructors must have a clear definition of what a value is and how it differs from value indicators.

Raths, Harmin, and Simon, in their book, *Values and Teaching*, have defined a value as having the following characteristics: (1) Cherished, (2) publicly affirmed, (3) freely chosen, (4) chosen from alternatives, (5) chosen knowing the consequences, (6) linked consistently with other values, and (7) acted upon.[8] These authors consider the following not to be values but only value indicators: (1) beliefs, (2) attitudes, (3) opinions, (4) feelings, and (5) morals. These *value indicators* differ from values in that they are guides that have not as yet met all the criteria listed for values.

An instructor can identify individuals with values from those not yet having attained them by the characteristics below.

Having Values	*Lacking Clear Values*
1. Proud	1. Apathetic
2. Enthusiastic	2. Inconsistent
3. Positive in their perceptions and reactions	3. Overconforming
4. Purposeful—have goals	4. Overly dissenting
	5. Confused
	6. Flighty—emotional personality. Tend not to give the impression that they are inwardly at ease.

In order for value clarification to be effective, Kohlberg recommends that teachers evaluate the developmental level of each student and adjust instruction so that the child is confronted with exciting and moral problems one stage above his developmental attainment. By doing this, the instructor facilitates the student's involvement. Kohlberg also suggests that the teacher confront students, when the situation arises, with their own illogic. In doing this, the teacher generally asks questions requiring students to search and identify certain concepts and principles they hold and their reasons for having them. The activities presented may provide structure or be unstructured depending on the needs of the students and the type of investigation. When two ethical principles are in con-

---

[7] Sidney Simon, Leland W. Howe, and Howard Kirschenbaum, *Values Clarification: A Handbook of Practical Strategies for Teachers and Students* (New York: Hart Publishing Co., 1972), pp. 20–21.

[8] Louis Raths, Merrill Harmin, and Sidney Simon, *Values and Teaching* (Columbus, Ohio: Charles E. Merrill Publishing Co., 1966).

flict, this is pointed out, and the students are asked to think of a higher ethic which would help solve the dilemma.

Simon's Value Clarification Method

Simon, unlike Kohlberg, has been less interested in research but more concerned with developing techniques of value clarification for students and teachers. He not only considers the cognitive processes of moral attainment but also of feelings and emotions of the person. In fact, many of his seventy-nine strategies are concerned with techniques involving feelings and emotions.[9]

Simon, like Piaget, believes that morality cannot be taught directly but that the students, through active involvement, social interaction, and the use of their minds, must actively mediate out moral principles. It is for these reasons that Simon and his colleagues have devoted considerable energy to translating Piaget's and Kohlberg's ethical theories into action through value clarification activities.

Fundamental to the clarification of values is a *positive self-concept*. The individual must feel that "I can be creative, do mathematics, write," "I am somebody" or, in other words, view himself as a capable, lovable human.

Conflict Involved

The typical value clarification strategy starts with some area of conflict where students are confused or have not as yet attained all the criteria outlined for a person having values. These areas might include such topics as:

1. Sex
2. Politics
3. Contribution of technology
4. Pollution
5. Religion
6. Family relations
7. Individual tastes
8. Culture—what is pleasing in the arts, music, etc.
9. Style—clothing, hair, etc.
10. War and peace
11. Race and other biases
12. Death
13. Authority—how much is needed?
14. Rules—which are necessary and why?
15. Society and what it does to the aging.
16. Personality—what is a desirable one?
17. Money—what does it do?
18. Success—what is a successful person?

Typically, instructors using value clarification strategies present problems which require students to identify their own values or resolve situations where two values may be in conflict. Students may be involved in researching the topic, discussing the problem in small groups or class discussions, and then summarizing their own views. Through the value clarification procedures, students should learn to:

1. Make choices when confronted with moral dilemmas.
2. Look at alternatives.

---

[9] Simon, *Value Clarification. . . .*

3. Consider thoughtfully the alternatives and the consequences of each of them. The instructor is supportive in helping students clarify arguments and challenges them to give evidence to support their views.

4. Consider what they cherish most relative to the problem area.

5. Publicly affirm their choices.

6. Behave and live their choices. The instructor strives to have students put their ideas into action.

7. Repeatedly examine patterns and behaviors in their lives.

General Suggestions

Other general suggestions for establishing a value clarification environment in the class are:

1. *Make the class student centered* rather than teacher centered. This can be done by dividing the class into groups consisting of four or five students and presenting a problem to discuss and resolve. Research indicates that *groups not led by teachers*, involving students in value clarification activities of high interest, achieve almost as well as those directed by teachers.[10] Piaget and Kohlberg both stress peer group participation because of the greater possibilities for development inherent in the socialization process. Social interaction requires the individual to perceive situations with different perspectives. In the process of playing different social roles in argument and resolving them, the individuals arrive at what is just.

2. *Involve students in role playing.* Encourage them to play various roles related to moral activities. They should be asked to try to make decisions anyone can live with, in other words, to learn the meaning of justice.

3. *Have students consider some situation where there are moral breakdowns,* as in mob rule. They should evaluate the situation and discuss how such a thing can be prevented.

4. *Invite students to discuss their behavior* in class, school, and community.

5. *Give responsibility* to students as much as feasible.

6. *Expose students to real as well as verbal conflicts,* for example, ask, "In what ways can we treat each other in this class so as to make everyone feel comfortable, welcome, and wanted?"

7. *Present conflict situations requiring students to interpret and use ethical principles* one level higher than their own.

8. *Guard against imposing one's ethical principles on students.* Remember their path in life is not your path!

9. *Bestow trust on students.* The more this is done, the more students feel obligated to fulfill this trust.

An example of using the above suggestions would be for a teacher to ask students if busing for racial integration is likely to achieve its objectives. The students would then have to make choices about the desirability of integration. It should be noted that students always have the right "to pass" in giving a response. The teacher may go on to present three or four integration plans and

---

10 Kohlberg, "From Is to Ought . . . ," p. 195.

have each individual rank in order the ones least to most desirable. The class then would vote on these to determine how they view the situation. This procedure allows students to express their beliefs on the issues and to consider alternatives. They may then be asked to study the consequences of their decisions. This discussion might initially end by the teacher's asking what the students are going to do personally to help solve the problem in their community. Later, the teacher might return to the problem after the students learned more about the topic and had chances to behave according to their decisions, to involve them further in the value clarification processes.

Value clarification can be introduced on the elementary school level, as part of the instruction in any secondary subject area, and as a special course.

More Examples of Strategy

An example of one value clarification strategy is called "Are you someone who . . . ?" In this strategy, each of the following questions is answered with a yes, no, or maybe. "Are you someone who:

1. likes to break the curve on an exam?"
2. likes to stay up all night when friends visit?"
3. will stop the car to look at a sunset?"
4. puts things off?"
5. will publicly show affection for another person?"
6. will do it yourself when you feel something needs to be done?"
7. will order a new dish in a restaurant?"
8. could accept your own sexual impotence?"
9. could be satisfied without a college degree?"
10. could be part of a mercy killing?"
11. is afraid alone in the dark in a strange place?"
12. is willing to participate in a T-group?"
13. eats when he is worried?"
14. can receive a gift easily?"
15. would steal apples from an orchard?"
16. is apt to judge someone by his appearance?"
17. would let your child smoke pot or drink?"
18. watches television soap operas?"
19. could kill in self-defense?"

(The instructor, as in all value clarification strategies, also does the task and may share his list after the students have enumerated theirs.)

This strategy allows a person to consider more thoughtfully what he values, what he wants of life, and what type a person he is. This exercise can be followed by "I am someone who. . . ."

The search for self, the who am I of life as a conscious act is a continual on-going process. As a person works and plays, this self-adventure becomes a touchstone for living. From knowing one's self, behaviors, patterns, etc., a new confidence, an internal security, a sense of potency emerges which is life-giving. Too often in our lives we search outside ourselves for meaning and become preoccupied with assigning blame and trying to change others. A life of meaning lies within each of us by discovering and cultivating what we are right now. Know what you prize and cherish and act on it as you live fully each day of your life.[11]

Another example of a value clarification approach using a *forced choosing* technique and a role approach is outlined below. In this type of lesson, students are presented with several choices and are then asked to select one or more of them.

Listed below are some of the discoveries Galileo made in his life.

a. Phases of Venus
b. Pendulum task
c. Moons of Jupiter
d. Speed of a falling body
e. Telescope development
f. Scientific experimenting using mathematics

g. Measuring using time
h. Construction of a water clock to prove acceleration
i. Construction of the first crude thermometer

If you were Galileo which would you think he thought was the most significant? Try to place your mind in Galileo's; you have just discovered the moons of Jupiter. How do you feel?

As Galileo being tried by the Inquisition, what ideas would go through your mind? How do you feel when the Inquisition condemns you for heresy and states the following:

"The first proposition, that the sun is the center and does not revolve about the earth, is foolish, absurd, false in theology, and heretical because expressly contrary to Holy Scripture. The second proposition that the earth revolves about the sun and is not the center, is absurd, false in philosophy, and from a theological point of view at least opposed to the true faith."

As Galileo, you did not behave like many Christians of your time in that when instructed by the church to desist learning and writing about science, you continued. Why do you thnk you had so much commitment about carrying on your investigations? Why do you think some men respect achievements in your time while others think they are heresies?

What lessons are to be learned from the trial of Galileo?

What relevance does this episode in history have for us today?

How do you think your perceptions may have evolved by doing this activity?

What do you need to do so as to become a more objective person and lessen the possibility of being bigoted?

If you were going to change this activity to make it more interesting or have a greater impact, what would you do?

Questions to Stimulate Ethical Development. Listed below are some examples of questions that may be used to involve students in clarifying their values.

---

[11] Sara Massey, "Value Activities," unpublished paper (University of Maine, 1972).

The instructor may present the question, involve students in discussion, and then have them research the topic before coming to a final decision. In carrying on discussions, teachers should use several types of questions, paraphrase and contrast answers among students, and maintain as much as possible an objective position, acting mainly as a moderator or clarifier.

1. Which of these do you prize the most?
2. What do you mean by that?
3. When that happens, how do you feel?
4. What other alternatives are there?
5. How have you demonstrated your commitment to that belief?
6. What evidence is there for that?
7. In what ways is that good or bad?
8. What do you feel like when you act like that during the situation and then later?
9. What if all people held the same view?
10. How certain are you that your belief is justified?
11. How would you enlist others to commit themselves to that goal?
12. How have you grown by being involved in this activity?
13. In what ways have you altered your opinion?
14. In what ways were you successful today, this week, etc.?
15. How do you feel about people playing "dominance games" where they are more interested in winning their point than in coming to agreement.
16. What situations indicate that a "dominance game" may have been going on in this discussion?
17. How do you rate yourself relative to being a manipulative person and what do you feel about this?
18. What would you define as a good life style and what are you doing to attain it?
19. If you were going to make your room or this room more pleasant, what would you change?
20. How would you change, for example, hospitals, prisons, police stations, county and state offices to make them more humanistic environments?
21. How does your present stand compare with the one you stated previously?
22. Why should there be courts?
23. What do you think about those people who deliberately broke the law to help the slaves?
24. If you were an Arab, what arguments would you propose relative to solving the Israel-Arab problem? If you were an Israeli, what arguments would you propose? If you were head of a United Nations delegation to mediate the problem, what would you propose?
25. Why have universally free education? Why not select those students who are the most gifted scholastically, educate them, and put the others to work?

Example—Value Clarification in Biology

An example of how value clarification can be integrated with a secondary biology course is outlined below.[12]

Selection and Sequencing of Biologic Content and Related Social Issues

---

Biologic Content	Social Issue
1. Flow of matter and energy	1. Should solid refuse be disposed of in landfills?
2. Relation of organisms to each other and their environment	2. Should we continue the use of pesticides to control agricultural pests?
3. Population growth and regulation	3. Should the human race be considered too populous?
4. Succession	4. Should humans continue the use of strip mining?
5. Cellular structure and diffusion	5. Should abortions be allowed?
6. Foods and respiraton	6. Should Americans question the nutrition of the foods they eat?
7. Cellular multiplication	7. Should drugs that cause chromosomal damage be allowed?
8. Synthesis of carbohydrates and proteins	8. Should food shortage be allowed to control the size of the human population?
9. Gamete formation	9. Should we allow the use of mutagenic agents?
10. Mendelian laws	10. Should geneticists be allowed to alter the genes of humans?
11. Natural selection	11. Should the minority have rights over a majority when the minority's health is involved?
12. Reproduction	12. Should we allow venereal disease to eliminate behavioral deviants?
13. Development	13. Should society retain all congenitally defective persons at home?
14. Plants: classification and structure	14. Should we allow technologic progress to continue the destruction of natural plant life?
15. Animals: classification and structure	15. Should we be aware of how we determine when we die?
16. New Bubbleton's budget	16. Should biologic principles form the basis of a community's resolution of its social issues?

---

[12] Melba James, Edward Schmidt, and Thomas Conley, "Social Issues Serve as Unifying Theme in a Biology Course," *The American Biology Teacher* 36 (6) (September 1974): 347.

Summary

Piaget has revealed that as children mature cognitively so do they evolve to higher moral and ethical levels. Kohlberg using Piaget's work as a foundation has done longitudinal and cross-cultural studies of the ethical development of children. He too finds that there is an invariant order of these stages, they are hierarchical and progress to higher structures encompassing new sets of operations. The development includes six stages: (1) avoidance of punishment, (2) prudence, (3) fear of disapproval, (4) conformity to authority, (5) democratic and legalistic attitudes, and (6) universal compassion for life.

Kohlberg like Piaget has found that the development of stages is found in every culture so that it is universal. However, the rate of progression may vary according to socio-economic class and culture. He further found that the home is the most important influence on the development of morals and this is particularly so if the child experiences a "just" environment. The school, however, can and does effectively contribute to ethical development.

Simons and others have devised educational systems to help foster moral development. These methods and activities generally fall under the title of value clarification. Value clarification lessons involve conflict and selection of values from various levels and alternatives.

A holistic view of education should be devoted to aiding individuals manifest their total potential as humans. Students need to have opportunities to grow morally and ethically. For teachers to ignore this aspect of development is to decrease their effectiveness as educators.

Now go to MEDIAPAK F. When you have completed it, return to this text and take the Self-evaluation Inventory for this chapter and MEDIAPAK F.

Self-evalution Inventory

Directions: Listed below are some of the main topics covered in this chapter and MEDIAPAK F. Read each statement and rate it on the scale TWICE: once according to what you knew about the topic before starting this part of the program and again according to what you have learned after completing it. Circle the appropriate number and mark B for before and A for after next to it, as indicated below:

Topic	Student Evaluation					
	Low	Moderate			High	
Example: Important Piagetian mental operations.	①B 2	3	4	⑤A 6		
1. Piaget's levels of moral development	1	2	3	4	5	6
2. Characteristics of Kohlberg's six stages	1	2	3	4	5	6
3. Characteristics of avoidance of punishment stage	1	2	3	4	5	6
4. Characteristics of prudence stage	1	2	3	4	5	6
5. Characteristics of fear of disapproval stage	1	2	3	4	5	6
6. Characteristics of conformity to authority stage	1	2	3	4	5	6
7. Characteristics of democratic or legalistic stage	1	2	3	4	5	6
8. Characteristics of universal value of life stage	1	2	3	4	5	6
9. The developmental character of Kohlberg's theory	1	2	3	4	5	6
10. The universal significance of Kohlberg's theory	1	2	3	4	5	6

11. How Kohlberg's stages correlate with Piaget's levels	1	2	3	4	5	6
12. The importance of a just environment	1	2	3	4	5	6
13. The characteristics of adolescents in reform schools	1	2	3	4	5	6
14. The implication of Kohlberg's theory for prison populations	1	2	3	4	5	6
15. The ethical attainment of orphans	1	2	3	4	5	6
16. The percentage of adults who attain formal thinking	1	2	3	4	5	6
17. The percentage of adults who attain Kohlberg's stage 6	1	2	3	4	5	6
18. The fact that individuals do not always behave at one level	1	2	3	4	5	6
19. The role of value clarification in helping students cognitively develop	1	2	3	4	5	6

Now that you have assessed your growth after reading this chapter and viewing MEDIAPAK F, review those areas above where you indicate there is either a lack of growth or confidence about the topic.

You are now ready to review the text and take the final self-evaluation inventory in the appendix. It is suggested that you also consult the appendix for suggestions for further reading related to Piaget's theory.

How to
Administer Piagetian
Interviews   10

In the three chapters that follow, tasks are suggested for determining whether or not a child has achieved the level specified. Each of the tasks to be administered outlines a basic structure for the interview. Feel free, however, to modify them so as to make hypotheses about the child's thinking during the interview. Note that no interviews are suggested for the sensory-motor stage because children of this period have to be observed to identify their level. If you are particularly interested in this stage, refer to the chapter on the sensory-motor period for suggestions of things to note. Certain specific suggestions for giving the tasks should be followed:

1. *Establish Rapport:* It is important that the person giving the interview establish good rapport with the child before administering the tasks, i.e., ask her name, age, etc., as suggested on the interview form which follows. Tell her you have some games to play, and all answers are acceptable. You might state further that what you want to find out is how children perform the tasks and what they think of them or that you are also trying to develop your ability to ask questions and find out how better to interview. Try to make the tasks fun to do, smile a lot while the child does them, and do what you can to lessen the child's feeling that the interviews are a threatening experience. Above all, attempt to avoid giving the child the impression that she is a guinea pig in the session.

2. *Do Not Give Answers: Do not* tell the child she is wrong or right, just accept her answer and either you or an assistant record them on the Piagetian child interview form.

3. *Ask for Justification:* Always ask for the justification of an answer. Do not assume if a child gives a correct answer she has done the proper thinking. In the interview we are interested in determining how the child thinks, i.e., is she really conserving, not just whether or not she gives a correct answer.

4. *Hypothesize about the Child's Thinking:* Formulate in your mind certain hypotheses about how the child is thinking. Ask the child questions to test your hypotheses to

This chapter should be reviewed each time before administering interviews.

determine whether or not they are correct. Remember you are interested in determining the child's perceptions and rational processes and to do this may require asking several questions.

5. *Use the "Another Child Told Me" Approach:* In asking the child to justify an answer, you may ask why she thinks it is correct. It has been my experience that some children will not respond to why questions. I suspect that they often consider it to be rather threatening to have a teacher, etc., ask such a question because they might fail. Generally, however, if you restructure your questions giving an episode like the following, they will respond:

"The other day a boy told me that the rolled out clay in the form of a hot dog weighed just as much as the clay before it was changed. What would you say to him? How would you prove his answer was right or wrong?"

6. *Allow for Wait-time:* Remember that most tasks require some form of logical-mathematical reasoning. These take time for the child to do mentally. Therefore, do not rush the child in your interview. Allow her time to think, five or more seconds time allowance is not too much. This is hard for most teachers to practice because studies have shown they usually allow only one second on an average for a student to respond.

7. *Have Fun:* Most of all, have fun giving the tasks and try to see that children have similar experiences.

Starting on page 120 is an interview form which can be copied and used to note the task achievement of the child. It will probably be best for you to record the responses on this form after, rather than during, the interview or have another person assist you by recording the responses while you interview. The individual doing this should appear disinterested in the interview and act as though he is involved in something else so as to make the child more at ease.

The interview form needs some clarification. In each session you should *plan on giving several tasks,* seven or more to preoperational and concrete-operational children, five or more to formal-operational children. The time for administering these will vary from twenty to forty minutes, depending on the age and cognitive level of the child.

Place a description of each task in the left-hand column. Check in the appropriate column whether the child achieved or did not achieve the task. In the third column write the stage the child attained. For example, if a child of four achieved multiple classification, you would write preoperational.

With many children, you will not get a clear demarcation of stage. They might perform preoperationally on six tasks and concrete operationally on two. If this is the case, how would you classify a person according to stage as indicated on the interview form? You probably would mark the transitional square on the basis of your limited interviewing measures.

One additional note of advice, occasionally in the interviewing procedure, a child will not, for example, conserve substance but later on conserve weight, which is at a more advanced level of cognitive development. The previous notations on the interview form will quickly indicate this to the interviewer. The interviewer can then design another conservation of substance task later in the session and give it to the child. Often children achieve a level the second time but not the first. The fact that this occurs is probably due to the child's adjusting to the interview situation.

A last bit of advice—have fun administering your interview but be cautious about your interpretations. Remember administering the tasks does give you insights into the child, but they are small measures for what is big and complex —a human.

Piagetian Interview Form*

Name of Child ——————— Interviewer's Name ——————— Location ————

Age ——— Grade ——— Sex ——————— of child.

Activity description, e.g., conservation of substance, class inclusion, etc.	Achievement: + Task achieved — Non-Achieved	Indication of cognitive level, e.g., preoperational. Note: If child doesn't achieve level of task, it is assumed he is at a lower level.
1.		
2.		
3.		
4.		
5.		
6.		
7.		
8.		
9.		
10.		

How many tasks were achieved: preoperational ——— concrete-operational ———

formal-operational ———?

Piagetian Interview Form (cont'd.)

According to Piaget, indicate below how you would classify this individual:

Check one

1. Preoperational—2–7 years ☐

   Transitional ☐

2. Concrete-Operational—7–11 years ☐

   Transitional ☐

3. Formal-Operational—11–14 years ☐

NOTE: Transitional means the child is in transition from one stage to another. If a child achieves some tasks but not others on the same level, she probably is between stages of development as characterized by Piaget.

List below any general comments you may wish to make related to the interview:

To be more certain of your above classification, what would you do?

How did administering the interview affect your perception of children?

Piagetian Interview Activities for the Preoperational Level 11

Multiple Classification

The answers which are not acceptable as justifications for the tasks in this chapter are:

1. No answer.
2. Wrong answer or no correct justification.
3. Magical type of response, for example, in the class inclusion task below, if the child says there are more red beads than wooden beads because red beads are prettier than blue beads or there are more red beads than wooden beads because they are brighter.
4. Reliance on authority, for example, my brother told me so.
5. Description of procedure, for example, in the class inclusion task below, if the child says there are more red beads than wooden beads because you placed them on the string first.

Place in front of a young child (age four or five) two small boxes and several shapes of paper such as circles and squares. There should be two different sizes of each of the shapes. Half of the shapes should be red and half blue. Ask the child to put all the shapes that go together in one box and all the other shapes in another box. How do you think the child will first group the shapes? Why? After they have done this, put all the shapes back on the table and ask the children to group the objects in another way.

Discussion: The children will probably group the objects first by color. The second time they may do it by shape. Some children may start to group the shapes one way and then in the middle of doing this, change their approach. They are confused about the criteria they are using. This task requires multiple classification ability—realizing there is more than one way to group things. Children of this age usually can do this fairly well.

Class Inclusion

Place several wooden beads in a dish. All of the beads except two should be the same color, for example, two yellow, the rest red. You may substitute colored straws cut into inch-long pieces for beads. Ask a child four to six, "Are there more red beads or wooden beads?" What do you think these children will say? Why?

Next ask, "If I were to string the beads to make a necklace, would the necklace be longer if I used all the wooden beads or all the red beads? Why?" What will the child say? Why? What responses do you think a concrete-operational child would make? Why? Try this activity with concrete-operational–aged children to find out.

Discussion: This is a class inclusion task in classification. Children of four or seven have difficulty realizing that what is said about the class is true of all of its members. They are overcome by perceptions—the number of red beads strikes them more than the fact that all the beads are made of wood. They may say, therefore, that there are more red beads than wooden beads. Piaget has found that the nature of the objects used in this task influences the results. For example, if you ask children even up to age seven or eight who are looking at several pictures of the cat family, with more pictures of tigers, whether there are more tigers than cats, they may not perform this correctly.

Class Inclusion

Show the children some fruit, for example, ten raisins and two apples. Ask, "In what ways are these alike? What do you call them? Are there more raisins than fruit? If I took the fruit and you took the raisins, would I have more, or you? How would you be able to prove who had more?"

Discussion: This activity tests again for class inclusion. Does the child realize that the subclass *raisins* is included in the major class *fruit*, or is he overcome by the perception of a large number of raisins?

Conservation Task

Show a rubber band to a child. Stretch the rubber band and ask, "Do I have more, less, or the same amount of rubber band as I had before I stretched it? Why?"

Discussion: Preoperational children do not conserve. They do not realize, therefore, that changing the shape of an object does not alter its mass. Also, try this activity with concrete-operational children and note the differences in their explanations.

To correctly indicate that children have achieved conservation they should give in the justification of their answers one of the following:

1. *Invariant Quantity*—state that nothing has been added or taken away from the material being conserved.

2. *Compensation*—indicate that something done to one part of the material is compensated for in another dimension. For example, in pouring water from a tall to a short, wide glass, the difference in the decrease in height is compensated for by an increase in the diameter or width of the glass.
3. *Reversibility*—state that if the substance were returned to the way it was originally, it would be the same.

Conservation of Substance

Obtain some putty, bread, cookies, or cake. Pinch off some of the material and ask, "Do I have more, less, or the same amount now as I had before?"

Discussion: If the child says you have more or less he does not realize that altering the shape of the material does not affect its amount. The child, therefore, does not conserve substance.

Conservation of Substance

Obtain some clay, make two round balls of equal size. Ask, "Are these two balls the same size?" If the child agrees, continue with the activity. If he does not agree, alter the putty until he thinks the balls are equal. Roll one of the balls into a hot dog or hamburger shape. Ask, "Do I have more, less, or the same amount of material now as when I started? Why? The other day a boy told me that there was more in the rolled out clay. How would you prove that he was right or wrong?"

Discussion: Children who think the flattened shape has more clay do not conserve substance. You can even put these on a balance before and after you roll the one ball of clay. They still will believe, if they are preoperational, that the flattened hamburger or rolled hot dog has more.

Young children think if you do something with an object, for example, change its shape, then its other properties (such as weight) also change. To conserve, children must realize in this task that rolling out the clay only changes its form. If a child does not achieve this task, modify it slightly. Pick up the elongated piece of clay. Take some clay from one end. Ask, "What have I done to the clay?" Then, add this pinched off portion to the middle of the elongated clay. Ask, "What have I done to the clay now? Do I have as much, more or less, clay in the hot dog as when I first showed it to you?" Some children who do not conserve might do so with this modification. Piaget says some children indicate conserving in this manner around 5½ whereas conserving without the interviewer's intervention usually does not occur until 6 or 7. The achievement with the help of the interviewer would indicate the child is in transition to fully conserving substance.

Conservation of Substance

Show the child Figure A on page 125; explain to him that these figures represent cakes. (You might obtain two cupcakes to make the task more realistic.)

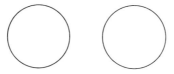

Figure A

Ask, "Are these the same or does one have more or less than the other?" Now show the child Figure B or cut one of the cupcakes as indicated below, placing

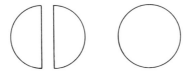

Figure B

it next to the first one. Ask, "Are the two cakes the same or does one have more or less? Why?"

Discussion: Preoperational children usually do not conserve substance. They will often say the cake that is whole has more because it still is together, or they will give some other type of illogical explanation.

One-to-one Correspondence

Obtain several objects that may be used as counters. These may be coins, bottle caps, straws, toothpicks, etc. You may want to prepare one group of stickmen for counters to make the activity more interesting. Line the counters up as indicated in Figure A and show them to the child. Ask, "What can you say about the

Figure A

length of the two rows? Are there more stickmen than straws or are they the same?" Take one of the counters out as indicated in Figure B. Ask, "What can

Figure B

you say about the length of the two rows now? Is there the same number of stickmen as straws, or does one row have more or less than the other?" Add a counter and rearrange them as shown in Figure C. Ask, "What can you say about the two lines? Are they the same or does one have more or less than the other?" Have the children count each of the lines and ask, "What can you tell me about the lines? Is there more, less, or the same number of objects in each?"

Figure C

Discussion: This task requires the student to do one-to-one correspondence. This means that he must note that for every counter there is in one row, there is one in the other row. Preoperational children in transition to the concrete stage usually center on the length of the rows. If the two lengths of the lines are the same, the children are perceptually impressed by this and say they are equal. Having them count the objects in each of the lines and then answer the question about the equal number in each line does not seem to help. This is so because preoperational children think from situation to situation, i.e., count the counters in each of the lines, without relating them. As a consequence, they can count five counters in one line and four in another and still say the lines are the same length.

One-to-one Correspondence

Obtain eight match sticks. Line them up as shown below. Ask, "Is each of

these lines the same? Why?" Alter the matches as follows. Ask, "Are the two

lines the same? Why? Is there more, less, or the same number of matches in each line? Why?"

Discussion: See previous task for discussion.

Number

Have a child count your fingers, one through ten. Then ask, "If the tenth finger is ten, what is the number of the finger on which you started counting?"

If this is 10, what is this?

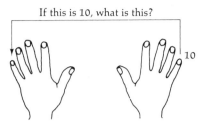

Discussion: Preoperational children often can count but do not know number. To know number they must be able to classify—realize all fingers are fingers— and order—place the fingers in a series keeping in mind that where the finger is in the series determines its number. The child must further realize that he has to disregard the object differences, in this case the finger variation, while still grouping them together. He must also understand that the number is not just the name of something but signifies its place in an order and represents how many objects are present. If children know and understand the meaning of number, they are probably in transition or are concrete operational.

Successive States vs. Transformations

Obtain a straw. Hold it erect and have a child watch it fall. Ask the child to make a series of pictures to show how the straw fell. After doing this, show the child several cards as illustrated below and ask him to place the cards in order.

Discussion: Preoperational children usually center on *successive states* of changes rather than on the transformations made in changing. As a consequence, they usually will get the first and the last picture in the series correct but mix up the others. To accurately place the pictures in order, they would have to hold a moving picture impression of their observation in mind and apply this to ordering the cards properly. Their minds are not capable of doing this.

Perception Bound

Give a child two pictures, one showing a large stick figure (6½ inches long), and another showing a smaller one (6 inches long). Tell the child, "These boys are twins. They were born on the same day at the same time." Ask, "What can you tell me about the boys? What can you say about their ages?" If they say the larger figure is older, tell them that the larger figure was born after the smaller one. Point to the cards again and ask, "Which one is older?"

Show the child two other drawings, one of a boy and one of a girl who is taller than the boy. Tell the child, "The girl was born in 1950, and the boy in 1949." Ask, "Which one is older?"

What would you do as a teacher to help the child build better concepts of age and time?

Discussion: Since preoperational children are preception bound, they are fooled by visual impressions. They do not use their minds as much as children in the next stage to verify whether what they see is correct. As a result, the child is likely to think the taller figures are older. He confuses height with age. To help children gain better understanding of these concepts, have them measure each other and determine the height of all their friends or pupils in a class. Have them cut out strips of newspaper to represent the height of each pupil and other strips of paper to represent age in years and months. These can be used as bar graphs, as indicated below. Activities of this type should help children to eventually gain a better realization that height does not necessarily correlate with age. Remember, however, that the child has to come to this realization; it will do you no good to tell him this.

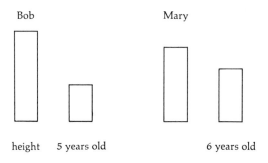

Bob   Mary

height   5 years old   6 years old

Relating Change

Show the child the diagram below or the apparatus and ask, "What will happen to the length of string A when weight is put on it? What will happen to the B length of string? Will the change in the B length be more, less, or the same as A? Why?"

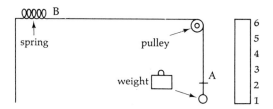

Discussion: Children of this period will realize that A will get longer and B will get shorter. However, since the child cannot think in quantitative terms, he usually thinks the gain in A is more than the loss in B.

Art, up to age four

Obtain some colored paper, cut out or draw the following shapes. Ask the children to copy the drawings.

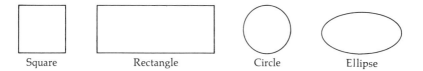

Square	Rectangle	Circle	Ellipse

Discussion: Children up to age four usually draw all the lines as curved and closed.

Art, ages two through five

Draw on a piece of paper the shapes below. Ask the children to draw what they see.

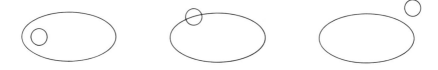

Discussion: Children as young as age three will demonstrate that they recognize that an object may be inside, on the line, or outside the eclipse.

Structure, Transitional, ages four through seven

Construct two small cardboard squares three inches by three inches, place them as shown in Figure A. Ask the child to draw what he sees in Figure A. If he draws it correctly, proceed to the rest of the activity. If not, stop and do some other activity. Failure to do this first task indicates the child has not yet reached

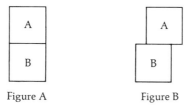

Figure A	Figure B

the transition to the concrete level. For those who can draw Figure A, ask, "How would A look if it were slid slightly to the right of B but were still on top of it?" (see Figure B) After the child makes his diagram, push A as shown in Figure B. Have the child draw what he sees.

Discussion: By age 7, 77 percent can draw Figure B correctly before seeing it done. By age 5½, only 76 percent can actually make a simple copy of Figure B when seeing it. Children around age 5 will often draw the diagram in Figure B as shown in Figure C, following.

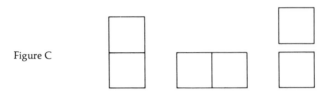

Figure C

At a slightly higher stage they draw Figure D. The progression of the ability of the children to improve in their representation of the squares and the prediction of what happens illustrates an advancement of mental structuring with age.[1]

Figure D

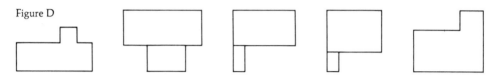

Conservation of Weight, Transitional

Obtain some clay. Roll it into a ball, then in front of a child divide it into several small pieces. Ask, "Do all these pieces weigh more, less, or the same as the original ball? Why? How would you know for sure? What would you do to find out?"

Discussion: Preoperational children do not conserve weight. They may think the little bits of clay press more on a balance and, therefore, weigh more. This activity may be altered and further tested by forming two clay balls of equal size and weight. Weigh them in front of the child so he sees that they are equal. Take one ball and make it into several small pieces. Ask, "What do you think will happen to the balance if the little clay pieces are hung from the balance in various ways?" (as shown below) Perform this activity and ask, "What happened?

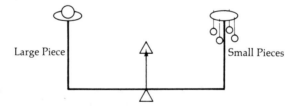

Large Piece   Small Pieces

Why?" You might ask, "What happens to the weight of a baseball while it is going through the air compared to when it sits at rest?" Children at this stage often think a body in motion weighs differently than at rest.

Space-Distance

Place two dolls or other objects at opposite ends of a board about eighteen inches long. Place a brick about halfway between them. Ask, "Are the dolls the same distance, farther, or closer, apart than before I placed the brick between them?

---

[1] For further information see Sinclair, "Different Types of Operatory Structures," in *Cognitive Development Research and Mathematical Education,* eds. Myron Rosskopf, Leslie Steffe, and Stanley Taback (Washington, D.C.: NCTM, 1971), pp. 53–65.

Why? If I take the brick away will the dolls be closer, farther, or the same distance from each other?"

Discussion: Children not having a good understanding of distance will say that the dolls are closer because the brick takes up some space. This has great implications for primary teachers when working with linear measurement. They must realize that the child's concept of distance is different from that of the adult. Placing a divider between objects changes the distance to the child.

Perception of Liquid Level, to Concrete, up to ages nine through ten

Obtain a bottle and tip it in several positions. Then prepare the diagram shown below. (Note: If you are going to evaluate several children, duplicate your drawings.) Ask children to draw in each of the bottles how the water would look if the bottle were half-filled.

Discussion: The children will respond something like the following:

1. The early preoperational stage child scribbles all over the bottle.
2. A child in the next development level will draw the liquid parallel to the bottom of the bottle.

3. A child in the next stage will draw the liquid obliquely toward the opening.

4. Children ages nine through ten draw the water levels correctly.

Artificialism

Ask a child, "Who made the sun? Who made the stars? Who made the moon? Who made the mountains? Who made the space ship that went to the moon? Who made a waterfall, lake, ocean waves?"

Discussion: Preoperational children believe in artificialism. They think all phenomena are made by humans or God. (God to them, however, is just a big person). Young children, for example, will say that the sun was made from a big fire started by people.

Realism

Ask a child the following questions:
"What is his name? Why does he have that name?"'
"If he didn't have that name, would he be the same person?"
"If a cat weren't called a cat, would it still be the same animal?"
"Have you ever had a dream? Where did it come from?"
"Did the things you dreamed really happen?"
"Who causes dreams?"
"When you have a dream where is it?"

Discussion: A child of this stage believes that everything he perceives has the same reality. The child believes, because of his egocentrism, that the way he sees things is the way they *really* are for everyone. Names of objects are real and are an integral part of the thing named. The child thinks that, if the name is taken away, the object will not exist. He believes that he could only be called one name and would not be the same person if given another name. Only as the child nears the next stage does he realize that a name is not intrinsically a part of an object or a person. Children further believe that dreams are occurrences that really happen. They think dreams are caused by the people they dream about and that these people actually are present in the room or bed during the dream and not in their heads.

Animism

Collect several objects, buttons, broken buttons, flowers, coins, rocks, straws, toys, pencils, chipped dishes, and pictures of waves, clouds, animals, trees, crystals, grass, etc. Place these in front of the child. Ask, "What does it mean to be alive? Is a dog alive? How do you know?" Then point to each of the objects and ask the child if it is alive or not. Break some of the objects and ask the child if it is still alive and why or why not.

Discussion: Preoperational children are characterized by animism. This means they attribute living qualities to all kinds of things. They believe that most things are alive and have a purpose similar to other organisms.[2]

Time to Time and Size Relationship

Prepare two ordered series of seven drawings each: one series of orange trees and the other of apple trees. Make the apple tree drawings larger than the orange

---

[2] For further information on this topic and a standardization test see W. Dennis, "Piaget's Questions Applied to a Child of Known Environment," *Journal of Genetic Psychology* 60 (1942): 307–20.

trees up until the fifth one, then make the orange trees larger. Tell the child that these drawings represent the growth of two trees over several years. The apple tree when planted was one year older than the orange tree. Have them look at the drawings of the trees. Point at each of the pairs of fruit trees in order from small to large. Ask, "Which one of these trees is the older?"

Discussion: Children ages seven through nine have difficulty separating time from size. If something looks larger to them, it is considered older. By the ninth year, children usually develop a mental structure correlating duration with certain events.

Time, Duration, Length of Time Intervals

Obtain a watch with a second hand. Rap on a desk rapidly for a minute, watching the watch, but not giving the impression that you are noting time. Rap again on the desk, but much slower for a minute. Ask, "Which took more time, the first or second series of raps I made on the table?"

Discussion: Children up to age seven believe quick activities take longer. They relate more raps on the table as taking more time because there are more of them. Piaget reports that children do not understand how a clock works in measuring time until age seven or eight. In order to do this, they must understand that each second on a clock is equidistant and that ten seconds of time means the clock's second hand moved ten spaces. Knowing what you do about children's conception of time, at what grade would you teach it?

Construction of Two-dimensional Space, to Concrete-Operational, up to age nine

Obtain two pieces of regular-sized typing paper. Place a dot on one piece of paper about halfway from the top and halfway from the center of the sheet. Place rulers, pencils, string, and scissors next to the papers. Ask, "How well can you place a dot on the blank sheet so that it is in the same location as the one on the other sheet?"

Discussion: The young preoperational child will guess at where the dot should be placed and will not use the rulers. More advanced preoperational children will take a ruler but use it to make only one measurement, i.e., from the top, bottom, or side. They are usually surprised that this does not give them the correct location. Usually by age nine, children make two measurements and coordinate these to exactly locate the placement of the dot. By so doing, they indicate they grasp the concept of the axis of coordinates. This knowledge is later essential to understanding higher mathematical concepts in Euclidean geometry.

Successive Order of Objects and Reversing, ages four through six

Obtain a hollow cardboard cylinder such as commercial paper is rolled on and three different colored marbles. Make a cardboard runway that fits inside the cylinder to roll the marbles along it. Place the marbles on the cardboard runway in order. Ask, "If I push these marbles on the runway, in what order will they come out the other side of the tube?" Push the marbles. Ask, "In what order do you think the marbles will come out if I push the marbles back through the tunnel?"

Discussion: Most preoperational children beyond age four will state the proper order for pushing the marbles through the tube. Children up to age six, however, have difficulty in reversing the order.

Speed, ages four through six

Obtain two hollow cardboard tubes such as come with sandwich wrap. Cut one tube to be a few inches shorter than the other. Obtain two small figures or markers of different colors that can pass through the tunnels. Line the tunnels up so that one of their ends are even. Place the markers at the entrance of each of the tunnels where they are lined up unevenly. Ask, "If each of these markers were to enter the tunnels at the same time and come out the tunnels together, would they both be moving at the same speed?" Ask, "What do you notice about the tunnels? Are they the same length?" Move the markers through the tunnels to come out the other ends at the same time. Ask, "Did the markers move at the same speed?"

Discussion: Piaget believes ordering is basic to understanding speed. Young children believe if something moves past another object, it must be going faster. They do not take into consideration the differences in distance traveled. Objects that end together must be going at the same speed even though they covered different distances. Children eventually develop the concept of speed as being related to distance traveled per unit of time.

Speed

Obtain two toy cars of different colors or use markers. Draw on a piece of paper a line to indicate the end of a race. Place one of the cars behind the other. Move both of these cars with each of your hands so that they come to the finish line at the same time. Ask, "Which of the cars was going faster, or did they both move the same? How do you know? How about the distance traveled? Did one cover a greater distance? When was one car ahead of the other? Why? Which one moved faster? Just before they finished the race, which was going faster, or were they the same? Why?"

Discussion: Young children believe if the cars finish the race together, they must be moving at the same speed. This is because they confuse order, being in front or together, as indicating speed. Usually at age nine or ten children take into consideration where an object started and stopped, distance traveled, and the time it took. For example, they might say, "Both of these cars start and stop together but one covers a greater distance, therefore, it must have gone faster." If the child does not grasp this realization, he will have difficulty doing mathematical speed problems. This may occur even into the fifth and sixth grades. If a child cannot do such problems, use toy cars and other objects to help him discover the relationships of speed to time and distance so that he eventually will understand speed = distance/time.

Memory and Seriation

Obtain several sticks. Make a series of ten sticks starting with a stick one centimeter long and increasing their length as shown below. Have the child look at the sticks and tell him to remember how they are arranged. After the child has had sufficient time, take the sticks away and ask him to draw what he saw.

Repeat the activity a week later. If you have time and the opportunity, repeat the activity six months later.

Discussion: Children will vary in how well they can recall the information, as indicated by the results below:

Age	General Results	Arrangement of Sticks
3–4	Draws several sticks more or less all equal in length.	ǀǀǀ
4–5	May include sticks paired small then large. Draws sticks arranged three or four in a group.	ǀǀǀǀǀ ǀǀǀǀ ǀǀǀǀ ǀǀǀǀ
5	Draws correct seriation but not enough sticks.	ǀǀ'ǀǀ
6–7	Draws correct seriation and number.	ǀǀǀǀǀǀǀǀǀ

There is a high correlation between children's being able to perceive seriation and to note that the objects they see are also heavier, longer, shorter, wider, thinner, darker, etc. The ability to seriate is also dependent upon the kinds of materials used and the type of seriation. Seriation of length, for example, occurs about two years earlier than seriation of weight.

Piagetian Interview
Activities for the
Concrete-Operational Level **12**

Transition to Concrete-Operational, Time and Distance, up to age nine

Tell the child two men are walking at the same speed and distance, except one is walking in a straight line, as shown below. Ask, "Which one reaches his house

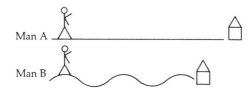

first? Why?" Also ask, "How does a watch run when a man runs fast compared to when he runs slowly?"

Discussion: Up to age nine, children usually have difficulty comparing the time taken and distance covered of two moving persons or objects. They believe going farther (in direction) takes more time. For this reason, preoperational and early concrete-operational children believe Man A will take more time. Furthermore, they do not realize that time can be measured independently of what has taken place, and they may think a watch runs according to how fast a person moves.

Seriation

Prepare ten cards of stickmen, dolls, flowers, or some animal so that they progressively increase in size. Place the first and last of the series on a table and tell the child to place the rest of them in order.

Discussion: During the concrete-operational period, a child develops her ordering ability. This ability usually occurs during ages seven and eight. Many children, however, even in the third grade, cannot do the task. If they cannot do it, they probably have difficulty with number because ordering is basic to understanding it, for example, the third finger is the third one in order. It is suggested that you also give the above task to a preoperational child and compare her approach to that of concrete-operational children.

Ordering

Show children, ages six through eight, stages of a developing moth, including the egg, larva, pupa, and adult. Discuss how the moth develops through these stages. Let the children look at the various stages of the organism and have them draw the stages in order of development. Next, show them a picture of one of the stages and ask, "What would be the next stage? What was the stage before this? Why do you think so?"

Discussion: If the children can do this and give reasons for their placement of the stages, they probably are able to order. Many young children will not be able to do this. The activity is still valuable because it helps children grasp some concept of development although they may not be able yet to interrelate them. If they do not order correctly, they probably do not see the stages as a continuum of an organism slowly progressing to maturity. Children unable to do this probably reason by transduction. In other words, they reason from specific situation to situation without interrelating them. They tend to look at each stage as a separate entity having little connection with the next. How would you determine if this is so? You might ask the child to tell you a story of how a moth develops.

Correspondence

Obtain a tall, slender jar, a transparent glass bowl, and some beads, pennies, beebees, or marbles. Place one bead (or object selected) in the jar and then one in the bowl. Do this several times saying each time, "I am placing one bead in the jar and now I am placing one bead in the bowl."

BOWL AND JAR WITH BEADS

Ask, "Do I have the same, more, or less beads in the jar as I have in the bowl? Why do you think so? "If the child does not give the correct response have her count the number in each container and then ask, "What do you think about the number in each now? Are there more, less, or the same?" If the child gives the correct answer and justification, you might repeat this activity but this time place the beads in a jar and a corresponding number in a sack so that they are not visible. Ask the same questions.

Discussion: This is a test to determine whether the child has developed the concrete-operational ability of being able to do one-to-one correspondence. If she can do this, she must realize that for every bead you put in the jar, you also have placed one in the bowl. The number of beads in one container must therefore correspond to the number in the other. Using the sack in the second activity insures that the child uses her mind and not just her perception to make conclusions.

Horizontal and Vertical Orientation

Tell the child there are ten children playing marbles. They are all going to try to hit a target marble. All players must be the same distance from the marble they are trying to hit. Show the child the diagram below. A black dot represents the target marble and a stick figure represents where one child would shoot from.

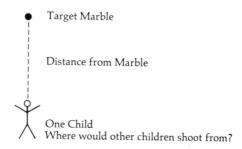

● Target Marble

Distance from Marble

One Child
Where would other children shoot from?

Give the child some other marbles or counters and tell her to put the counters where she thinks they should be placed so that each of the ten players has an equal chance of hitting the target marble. You may have to help the child by placing one marble so that you are sure she understands the task. After the child performs the task ask, "Why did you do it that way?"

Discussion: If the child places her marbles or counters roughly in a circle around the target marble, she probably has a good understanding of space and comprehends horizontal and vertical orientations.

Horizontal and Vertical Orientation

Obtain several counters. Draw two stick figures, one representing the teacher and the other a student. Place these figures some distance apart on a table. Ask the child to place the counters so that they are equidistant, halfway between the teacher and the pupil.

Discussion: The child should place the counters in a relatively straight line. Older concrete-operational children should demonstrate some use of mathematical reasoning when placing them on a line, by indicating that they have discovered it is a straight line, as shown below.

Straight Line ○———○———○

Reversibility

Have children grow bean seeds or show them plants in various stages of development. After they have raised some plants, have them draw how they grew. The children should diagram something like below. Give the children a diagram of a young plant and ask them to draw how it would look in stages before and after this picture. Next, have the children draw several pictures showing the stages of development of plants in reverse order. Ask, "Why do you think your pictures are true?"

Discussion: If they can reverse properly and give you reasons why they are drawing the plants in this order, they have probably achieved reversibility in their thinking. Checking for reversibility can be easily done whenever the children have prepared and learned something in one order and are then asked to reverse the order. For example, they have learned the states in a region of the United States from the north to south. Ask them to name the states from the south to the north. Try such tasks with preoperational children to note how they differ in this ability.

Reverse Seriation, may be difficult to age nine

Obtain twenty straws or make pictures of flowers or dolls. The straws should be cut so that you have two series of ten straws each that progress in length. If you use flowers or dolls, prepare two series of ten each so that they progress in size. Set up one series from short to long and then ask the children to take the other set and place them in reverse order (for example, they should place across from the largest doll the smallest doll.) In other words they should reverse the order.

Discussion: This task identifies whether or not children can reverse order of a series of objects. Children of seven can usually seriate, but many children ages eight through nine have difficulty in reversing the order.

Classification—Ascending and Descending Hierarchy

Prepare a number of cards, some labeled *birds* with birds on them, some labeled *ducks* with ducks on them, and some labeled *animals* with other animals on them. Show these to a group of eight- to ten-year-old children. Ask them to arrange the cards in groups according to each of the three labels. Next, place the "bird" pile on the "duck" pile and ask, "Is the bird label, now on top, still appropriate? Why?" Now place the "animal" pile on the others. Ask, "Is this appropriate? Why? Do all the cards belong in this pile? Are birds animals? Are ducks animals? If all the animals in the world died would there be any ducks? Why or why not?"

Discussion: This activity determines whether a child understands class inclusion, that is, ducks are not only ducks but also birds (an ascending hierarchy). Ducks are a subgroup belonging to birds, a higher major group. Asking if all the animals are killed would there be any ducks determines whether the child can also descend a hierarchy (go from animals, major group, to ducks, subgroup.) Descending a hierarchy is also a reversible operation because the child has to reverse the ascending process to a descending one. Interview several children of various ages on these tasks. They often differ significantly on their ability to do them.

Conservation of Area, ages eight through ten

Obtain eight cubes of sugar. Stack four together so that they appear as shown in diagram A below. Then, arrange the other four so they appear as in diagram B. Or prepare and show the child diagrams of the two situations. Ask, "Is the distance around (perimeter) A the same as around B? Why?" Tell the child, "The other day a girl told me they were not the same perimeter or distance around. What would you tell her? How would you prove it?"

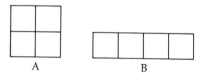

A   B

Discussion: By this age, children will usually conserve area but think if the area is the same so must be the perimeter. If each square were one inch wide, the perimeter of A would be eight inches and of B, 10 inches. If the child does not come up with correct responses, have her count the sides of each of the diagrams and then ask, "What do you think about the perimeters?"

Conservation, Transition to Concrete-Operational, ages six through twelve

Rip a newspaper in half. Ask, "Do I have more, less, or the same amount of newspaper as I had before?" (conservation of substance) Ask, "Do the combined pieces of newspaper weigh more, less, or the same as the paper did before it was torn? Why?" (conservation of weight) Ask, "If I put these torn pieces of newspaper in a large tank of water, would they occupy more, less, or the same amount of space as when the paper was whole? Why?" (conservation of volume) If you are not satisfied with the answers repeat this activity using two newspapers rather than one. Place both newspapers on a table. Ask the students if they agree that they are relatively the same. Leave one paper undisturbed on the table but tear the other one. Ask the questions above but have the children compare the torn one with the whole one on the table. For example, does the torn paper have more, less, or about the same amount of paper as the other one?

Discussion: Children do not develop conservation usually until after age six. In other words, they do not realize that physically altering matter does not change its amount, weight, or the volume it will occupy. Conservation of substance and weight usually develop by age eight, while conservation of volume occurs much later (around ages eleven to twelve).

Conservation of Displacement Volume

Obtain some clay and two jars filled three-fourths full of water. Divide the clay into two equal parts in front of the child and shape them into round balls. Ask, "Are these two balls equal?" If the child does not agree modify the balls until she does think they are the same, and then flatten one. Ask, "What do you think will happen to the water level of two equally filled jars of water if the round piece of clay is put in one and the flattened shape is placed in the other?" Before placing the clay in the jars, have the child mark on the sides of the jars with a crayon, pencil, or rubber band how the water levels will change. Place the clay in each of the jars. Ask, "What happened? What does that tell you? Why?"

Discussion: Conservation of displacement volume usually is not achieved until twelve years or older. Children who think altering the shape of clay changes its volume when immersed do not conserve volume. Elkind found only 47 percent of secondary students were proficient in conservation of displacement volume problems. However, there was a significantly higher level of achievement with an increase in age. Some formal individuals do not conserve this type of volume; what activities would you suggest to help them achieve it?

Conservation of Substance, Transition to Concrete-Operational, ages six or seven

Show a child a diagram of a kernel of popcorn and then draw a picture of it after it has popped. Ask, "Is there more corn after than before it is popped? Why has the volume changed?"

Discussion: Preoperational children, being perception bound, believe there is more corn to eat after it is popped. Concrete children know that altering the corn's state does not change its amount.

Part-Whole Relationship, Transition to Concrete-Operational, up to age nine

Ask the child, "Where is your town or city located? Is the state your town is in bigger, smaller, or the same size as the town or city? Are the people in your town also people in the state? Where do the people of your state live?" Draw a rough outline of a map of the child's state. Ask her to draw a rough outline of where she thinks some of the counties are in the state. Ask, "Are the people in these counties called by the name of the state? Are the people of your town also named after your state? Why do you think that? The other day a boy told me a San Franciscan is also a Californian. What would you tell that boy? How would you prove it?"

Discussion: The purpose of this task is to determine whether the child understands the parts—cities—are included in the whole—state. Often children may initially say that Denver, for example, is in Colorado but, when questioned, deny that Denverans are Coloradans. These children see parts and wholes as separate entities and have not, as yet, made the necessary rational relationship.

Number, Transition to Concrete-Operational, ages six through eight

Obtain ten straws. If a child can count, have her count them one through ten. Ask, "If the last straw is ten what is the number of the straw you started with?" Place the straws together and have the child count them. Move the straws apart. Ask, "Do I have more, less, or the same number of straws now?" Repeat this activity using fingers.

Discussion: Preoperational children often can count but do not know number. To fully comprehend number children must understand:

1. *classification*—realize that all fingers, although they do not look alike, are still fingers. In this case they must disregard object differences to constitute the set of fingers. They must also grasp the concept of cardinal numbers.
2. *cardination*—realize that no matter how you arrange objects in a set, you still have the same number.
3. *ordination*—place the straws or fingers in order and realize that where the object is in the order determines its number.

Physical Causality, Animism, Artificialism, Transition to Concrete-Operational, up to age nine

Ask questions about the following and how they were formed: lakes, wind, stars, floating objects, etc.

1. Stars: Ask, "What are stars? Where do they come from? How were they made? Why do you think that?"
2. Lakes: Ask, "When have you seen a large lake? What did it look like? How was it formed? What is a lake made of? What will the lake look like in a hundred years from now? Is a lake alive? Why do you think that?"
3. Wind: Ask, "Where does the wind come from? When it isn't here, where is it? Where did it come from in the first place? Where is it now? What makes up wind? How does the wind feel when it hits us? How do you feel when the wind hits you? Does it feel good or bad when it hits something? Is the wind alive? Why do you think that?"
4. Floating Objects: Ask: "What floats on water? Why do these things float? Do they like to float? Do they like to sink in the water? Why do you think that?"

If you are not satisfied with determining whether students give physical, animisitic, artificialistic, or magical explanations for these questions, ask similar questions for air, shadows, moon, sun, etc.

Discussion: Young children have a different view of reality compared to adults. They often give animistic, artificialistic, or magical explanations of phenomena in their environment. An *animistic* explanation is one indicating objects have qualities similar to animals, for example, conciousness, "The flower is sad." *Artificialistic* explanations state that certain physical entities are provided for human benefit, for example, "Water was made so we could drink it." *Magical* explanations are those indicating humans and/or a god causes physical events to happen, for example, "A man told the clouds to go away."

As children progress into the concrete-operational level, starting at ages seven or eight, they begin to replace these magical, artificialistic, and animistic explanations with those of physical casuality, for example, "Clouds go away because the wind blows them away." This indicates a significant advancement toward a better understanding of reality.

Class Inclusion, Transition to Concrete-Operational, ages six through eight

Show the children some fruit, for example, ten raisins and two pears. Ask, "In what ways are these alike? What do you call them? Are there more raisins than fruit? If I took the fruit and you the raisins, would I have more, or you? How would you be able to prove who had more?"

Discussion: This activity tests again for class inclusion. Does the child realize that the subclass *raisins*, is included in the major class *fruit*, and is the child overcome by the perception of a large number of raisins?

Piagetian Interview Activities for the Formal-Operational Level 13

Proportional Reasoning

This task assesses the student's ability to apply the concept of ratio and proportion. The student is given an 8½" × 11" card. Stickmen are drawn on each side
of the card, one being ⅔ the height of the other. The small and large stickmen
should be constructed to measure four and six jumbo paper clips, respectively.
Ask the student to measure the height of each of the stickmen with a set of eight

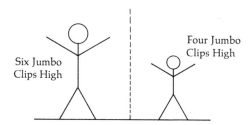

Six Jumbo
Clips High

Four Jumbo
Clips High

connected jumbo paper clips. After the student has measured and recorded the
heights of the two stickmen, the jumbo clips are replaced with a set of small
paper clips. Ask the student to measure only the large stickman with the new
set of clips. Then ask, "How tall does the small stickman measure, in terms of
small paper clips?"

Discussion: The measurement of the large stickman should be six jumbo clips
and nine small clips in length, and the small stickman should measure four
jumbo clips. The criterion for success on this task is the ability of the student to
accurately predict the height of the small stickman in terms of small clips (six
small clips). The student's justification must include a reference to direct ratio or

See the Observer Recording Form for Formal-Operational Interviews on page 150 for a sample
of how to record these interviews.

144

proportion. This is a simple proportion problem. The student may just guess and give you a number. If the child does, he is not demonstrating the use of formal thought. If, however, he tries to figure it on paper or reasons in a rational way, indicating that the situation is a simple proportion, he is demonstrating formal thought:

$$\frac{9 \text{ small}}{6 \text{ jumbo}} \times \frac{6 \text{ small}}{4 \text{ jumbo}}$$

Or the child could reason by dividing 6 into 9 that there need to be 1½ small clips for every jumbo clip.

Separation and Control of Variables

This task utilizes a simple pendulum consisting of a length of string thirty-six inches long and a set of varying weights. Ask the student to determine which variable or variables affect the frequency of oscillation of the pendulum (the number of swings per unit of time, for example, second). (Note: Since the length of the string is the only relevant variable, the problem is to isolate it from the others. Only in this way can the student solve the problem and explain the frequency of oscillations.)

Discussion: The criterion for success on this task is the student's ability to identify the one variable (length of string) that affects the oscillation of the pendulum. The student's justification must indicate that he *held all variables constant while manipulating only one variable* in reaching his conclusion. The student should initially indicate that variables involved in the problem could be weight, length of string, or height at which the pendulum is dropped. He may initially think a combination of these may affect the frequency. He may then describe a set of hypotheses and test these. However, before finishing he should *design an experiment controlling one variable at a time,* such as length of string, to find out whether his hypothesis is correct. In this way he should systematically eliminate the irrelevant variables. After completing the exercise, he should state the principle that the length of string determines the frequency, how fast it swings per second, and not the weight or height. The ability to plan experiments to separate and control, or manipulate, *one variable* at a time, observe it accurately, and make proper conclusions characterizes formal thought.

It is interesting to note that a preoperational child given the above pendulum problem just plays around with the apparatus and does not indicate any organized plan of attack.

A concrete child, however, shows an advance in that he may have a plan of attack—even obtain the correct answer. Nevertheless, he still is unsystematic in his approach in that he often does not control one variable, that is, he may change weight and length simultaneously and may make faulty conclusions.

Proportional Reasoning

The student is presented with a balanced scale consisting of a wooden rod with equally spaced numbered positions. Weights are attached as indicated in the diagram. Begin by using equal weights (ten grams) equidistant from the fulcrum (pivoting point). Remove one. Maintain equilibrium of the balance by holding the force arm. Ask, "Using any of the weights in front of you, how could you

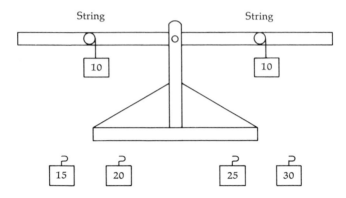

String   String

10   10

15   20   25   30

get the scale to balance?" After the student responds ask, "What other ways are there to balance the scale besides the one you chose?" Remove the weight from the scale. Place another weight nearer the fulcrum and maintain equilibrium by holding the force arm. Ask, "How may the scale be balanced by using the weights? How do you justify your responses?"

Discussion: The criterion for success on this task is the student's ability to equate length times weight on one arm of the fulcrum with length times weight on the other arm or to figure out the problem by using proportions. In order for the student to balance the scale he must apply the principle of levers.

Concrete children may realize that a small weight will balance a large one but do not indicate that the two functions of weight and length are related in a proportional manner as do formal thinkers.

Combinatorial Logic

Obtain five medicine droppers, baby food or other jars, and ten clear plastic cups. Prepare stock solutions of the following:

1. Dilute H_2SO_4—10 ml Conc. H_2SO_4 to 100 ml H_2O
2. Distilled H_2O
3. Hydrogen Peroxide—3 parts of H_2O_2 added to 97 parts H_2O
4. Sodium Thiosulfate—10 grams sodium thiosulfate to 1 liter of H_2O
5. Potassium Iodide—5 g to 1 liter H_2O

Pour the stock solutions into the baby jars as follows: jar 1, dilute sulfuric acid; jar 2, water; jar 3, hydrogen peroxide; jar 4, sodium thiosulfate; and jar 5, potassium iodide, labeled *g*. The student is then given the four jars containing colorless, odorless liquids which are perceptually identical. Then present him with two glasses, one containing solutions 1 + 3, the other containing solution 2. The contents of the glasses are *not* revealed to the student. Several drops from jar *g*

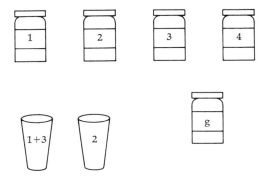

are poured into each of the two glasses. The student is asked to notice the re-actions. (The container containing 1 + 3 turns yellow, the other remains un-changed.) The student is told that the two samples were prepared from the jars and that each contains g.

Ask, "Can you reproduce the color?" Ten plastic cups are made available, and the student is allowed to attempt to reproduce the color. Record the student's procedure. If the color is successfully reproduced, ask questions to determine if he can identify the functions of each liquid. (The child should indicate that jar 2 does not alter the reaction one way or the other and jar 4 eliminates the color.)

Note whether the student performed the task as follows:

1. Made the color in one way. _____
2. Made the color in two ways. _____
3. Determined 1, 3, and g were necessary. _____
4. Determined 2 had no effect. _____
5. Determined 4 changed or prevented the color. _____

Discussion: The main criterion for determining whether the student is a formal-operational thinker is whether he establishes a *systematic procedure* for the role played by each of the solutions. Does he use, for example, a process of elimination? Does he realize that by combining 1, 3, and g the yellow solution occurs? If he cannot state these facts, but just goes about the activity by trial and error and does not indicate he understands the role of all the combinations, he is not a formal thinker.

Concrete-operational children differ from formal ones on this task because they usually combine two liquids at a time. After doing this, they no longer appear to be systematic in their investigations.

Syllogism

Prepare several syllogisms to see whether the student can use deductive logic, for example:

All mailmen wear purple suits.

John is a mailman.

Then he wears _____.

Bob is taller than Bruce.
John is shorter than Bruce.
Therefore, Bob is (*what to*) John?

Substitute symbols for words to see whether the student can use symbols well:

All *B*'s are *A*'s.
All *C*'s are *B*'s.
Then all *A*'s are _____.

Each syllogism consists of two premises and a conclusion. The student is presented with the syllogism and, after seeing it, is asked if it is a valid argument. For example: All milk trucks are white. Here is a white truck. Therefore, it is a milk truck. After the student responds that the argument is valid or invalid, he should be asked to justify his choice.

Discussion: The criterion for achieving on this task is the student's ability to successfully judge the validity of the arguments. In addition, the justification of each judgment must follow logical patterns of reasoning.

Syllogisms require deductive reasoning, an operational ability characteristic of the formal period. Research done at the University of Northern Colorado, however, suggests that students comprehend syllogisms to a much greater degree than they can the other tasks above.[1]

Concrete-operational children will not accept hypothetical situations which are not realistically true, for example, mailmen wearing purple suits. Formal-operational individuals, however, will accept "just suppose" situations.

Verbal Deductive Reasoning

Ask the following questions:

Bob is fairer than John.
John is darker than Bruce.
What is Bruce to Bob?

Discussion: If the student reasons correctly he should say that, from the information given, Bruce could be darker or lighter than Bob. If the student indicates he is reasoning correctly, the task has been achieved.

Hypothetical Reasoning

Show a student the following diagram of the top of a pool table. Ask him to trace how he would hit ball *y* so that it would collide with ball *x*, in each of the above positions, to make *x* go into one of the corner pockets. After he has drawn

---

[1] Daniel Ball and Steve Sayre, "Relationships between Student Piagetian Cognitive Development and Achievement in Science" (Ph.D. diss., University of Northern Colorado, 1972), p. 109.

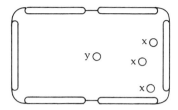

several ways he could hit the *y* ball, ask him to describe any rule that could be used in the future. You might have to help the student construct a rule. Ask, "If you hit the ball straight on, how will it move? If you hit it on a 45° angle, how will it move?" (You have to diagram a 45° angle to insure that he understands what it means.) Ask, "Can you compare the reaction of a ball bouncing off a wall with *y*'s reaction to *x*?"

Discussion: The student should, in his own words, state that the angle of incidence equals the angle of reflection. If the student does state this rule, he should explain the meaning to be sure he has not memorized it. He need not use the above words, as long as he can explain the law or state some rule. For example, for a ball bouncing off a wall, the student might say that if the ball comes in on an angle at a point four inches from the wall and six inches along the wall from the point where it is going to hit, it will bounce four inches away from the wall when it is six inches along it from the point it hit.

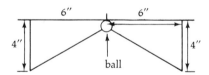

Memory Logical Reasoning

Set up an abacus, use counters, or draw the situation shown in the diagram. Tell

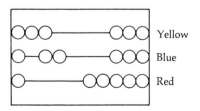

the student that he is to look at it and remember it later. Put it away. Have the student draw what he saw. Ask, "How did you insure you would recall this accurately?" Ask him to draw again what he saw a week, six weeks, etc, later.

Discussion: The student demonstrates formal thinking by describing a logical way to insure recall. For example, he might say, "There are three rows of counters—

each row has six. Row 1 is arranged 1 plus 5, Row 2 is 1 plus 2 plus 3, and Row 3 is 3 plus 3. The color sequence from the bottom is red, blue, and yellow."

When given the above task, preoperational children tend to make bizarre representations of the activity. This becomes less prevalent with concrete-operational children because they have better mental structures for handling the information.

Conservation of Volume

Ask formal-operational children, "How would you measure the volume of a fish? Why?" If they cannot understand this ask, "If you placed a fish in a transparent jar of water, how would that help?"

Discussion: If the students understand well conservation of volume, they should suggest immersing the fish in water and noting the change in water level. The amount of space the fish takes up in the water will result in a subsequent increase in the height of the water in the container. Another acceptable approach would be to fill a container with water. Lower the fish slowly into it and collect all the water overflow. The collected water equals the volume displaced by the fish.

Sample Observer Recording Form for Formal-Operational Interviews

Name _____ School _____

Class or Subject _____ Teacher _____

Sex _____ Level _____

Age_____ (yrs.) _____ (months) Info. X _____

Task 1—Proportional Reasoning

1. Predicted height of tall stickman. _____ Clips

2. Justification for prediction. _____

_____

_____

3. Classification of performance. _____

Notes:

Prepared by Daniel W. Ball and Steve A. Sayre.

Task 2—Separation and Control of Variables

1. Question: Which variable or variables affect the frequency of oscillation of this pendulum?

    Response: _____

    _____

2. Question: Can you design an experiment to prove that your choice is correct?

    Response: _____

    _____

Notes:

3. Classification of performance. _____

    _____

Task 3—Proportional Reasoning

1. Question: Using any of the weights presented here, how could you get the scale to balance?

    Response: _____

    _____

2. Question (Justification): How did you arrive at this answer?

    Response: _____

    _____

3. Question (Second situation): How could you get this scale to balance?

    Response: _____

    _____

4. Question (Justification): How did you arrive at this answer?

    Response: _____

    _____

    Classification of performance. _____

Notes:

Task 4—Combinatorial Logical Analysis

Record the procedure the student takes in solving the problem.

_____

_____

_____

_____

_____

1. Analysis of procedure. Check which one(s) of the following the student was able to do.

    _____1. Made the color in one way.

    _____2. Made the color in two ways.

    _____3. Knew that all of 1, 3, and g were necessary.

    _____4. Knew that 2 had no effect, or did not help or produce the color.

    _____5. Knew that 4 removed or prevented the color.

2. Classification of performance. _____

Notes:

Task 5—Syllogisms

1. After reading the syllogisms to the students, determine if their statements are valid or invalid.

               1. Justification:

Notes:

               2. Justification:

Notes:

Appendix A
Concrete-Operational
Reasoning Test

Directions: This test consists of thirty problems. Read each problem carefully before trying to answer it. Pick out the best answer from the choices given and write the number of your choice on a separate answer sheet.

1. Henry and Bobby decide to go to the ball park after school. They can't agree on which way to go, so Bobby goes one way (shown by the dotted line . . .)and Henry goes another way (shown by the dashed line - - -).

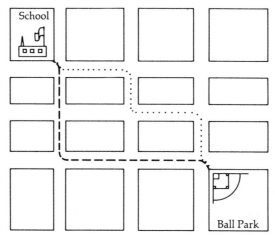

Which of these statements is true?
   1. Henry and Bobby will walk the same distance.
   2. Bobby will walk farther.
   3. Henry will walk farther.
   4. Impossible to say.

   Prepared by Paul Ankney and Lyle Joyce. From "The Development of a Piagetian Paper-and-Pencil Test for Assessing Concrete-Operational Reasoning" (Ph.D. diss., University of Northern Colorado, 1974).

2. The following box contains wooden beads. Fourteen beads are black and four are white.

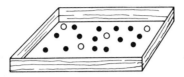

Are there more black beads than wooden beads?
   1. more black beads
   2. more wooden beads
   3. same number of black beads as wooden beads
   4. Impossible to say.

3. Two test tubes are filled with water. The water from tube *A* is poured into tube *X*. And the water from tube *B* is poured into glass *Y*, as shown following.

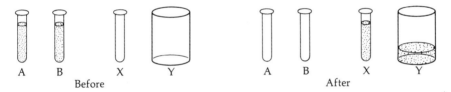

Which of these statements is true?
   1. *X* and *Y* both have the same amount of water.
   2. *X* has more water than *Y*.
   3. *Y* has more water than *X*.
   4. Impossible to say.

4.

What will the picture look like?

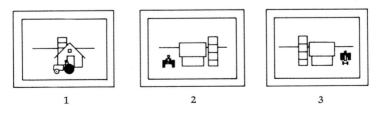

5. A farmer has two fields of the same size in which he wants to grow equal amounts of wheat. He plants wheat in a square plot in one field. In the other field this square has been divided into two parts, as shown below.

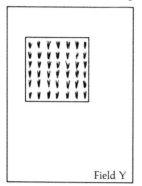
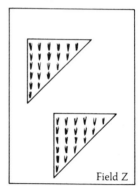

Field Y

Field Z

Which of these statements is true?
1. More wheat has been planted in field Y.
2. More wheat has been planted in field Z.
3. Field Y and Z are equal in the amount of wheat planted.
4. Impossible to say.

6.

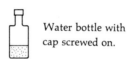

Water bottle with cap screwed on.

If the bottle is tipped as shown, which figure shows the correct water line?

1   2   3   4   5

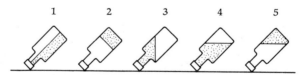

1. bottle 1
2. bottle 2
3. bottle 3
4. bottle 4
5. bottle 5

7. All the water from the short, fat bowl is poured into the tall, narrow glass.

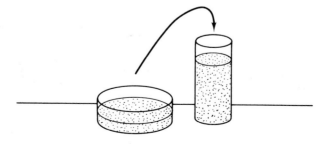

Which of these statements is true?

1. The water takes up less space now than it did in the bowl.
2. The water takes up more space now than it did in the bowl.
3. The water takes up the same amount of space in the glass as in the bowl.
4. Impossible to say.

8. Each man in this picture will be given the balloon most similar to himself in size. The largest balloon will go to the tallest man, and so on. Therefore, the man at the far left with the dark shirt will be given which balloon?

1. balloon 1
2. balloon 2
3. balloon 3
4. balloon 4
5. balloon 5

9. Playing with blocks, a girl builds a make-believe bird cage for a canary. Using all of the same blocks, she later makes a second cage.

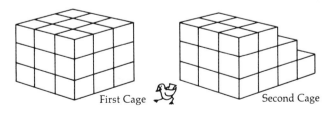

First Cage   Second Cage

Which of these statements is true about the amount of room that the canary will have for walking and flying?

1. The first cage has more space.
2. The second cage has more space.
3. The amount of room is the same in both cages.
4. Impossible to say.

10.

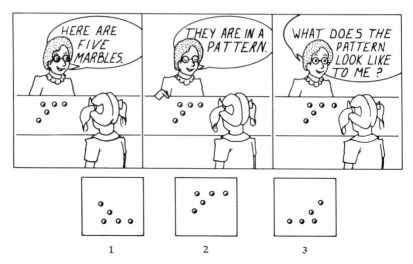

1   2   3

11. Sue likes candy better than ice cream. She likes ice cream better than soda pop. And she likes soda pop better than popcorn.

Which of these statements is true?
    1. Sue likes popcorn better than candy.
    2. Sue likes candy better than popcorn.
    3. Sue likes popcorn and candy equally well.
    4. Impossible to say.

12. Below are five Easter eggs. The youngest person gets the darkest colored egg, and so on.

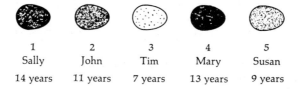

1	2	3	4	5
Sally	John	Tim	Mary	Susan
14 years	11 years	7 years	13 years	9 years

Which child would receive egg 1?
    1. Sally   4. Mary
    2. John   5. Susan
    3. Tim

13. Along the coast, are sea gulls more abundant than sea birds?

    1. There are more sea gulls.
    2. There are more sea birds.
    3. There are the same number of sea gulls as sea birds.
    4. Impossible to say.

14.

    1. car   3. block
    2. bottle   4. house

15. Look at the objects following. The pencil weighs less than the brush. The brush and the coin weigh the same. The coin weighs less than the shell.

Which of these statements is true?

    1. The pencil weighs *more* than the shell.
    2. The pencil weighs *less* than the shell.
    3. The pencil and the shell weigh the same.
    4. Impossible to say.

16. Which two lines in the box below run in the same direction and would never meet if they were drawn longer?

    1. *B* and *G.*
    2. *A* and *F*
    3. *E* and *F*
    4. Impossible to say.

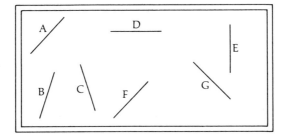

17. Mary and her friends went to the store and bought sacks of groceries as shown below. Each sack cost a different amount. The amounts were $5.50, $2.00, $9.00, $3.50, and $13.00.

Which sack of groceries would probably have cost $9.00?

    1. sack 1
    2. sack 2
    3. sack 3
    4. sack 4
    5. sack 5

18. Two joggers run around the paths shown below. They start together at *A* and *B*. Each runs for four minutes. They stop together at *X* and *Y*.

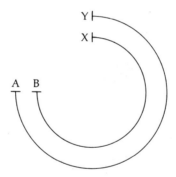

Which of these statements is true?

    1. The runner who started at *A* ran faster and had higher speed.
    2. The runner who started at *B* ran faster and had higher speed.
    3. The two runners had the same speed.
    4. Impossible to say.

19. The jar alone has a screw-on cover. A marble is suspended from the center of the cover, and then the cover is put on the jar as shown.

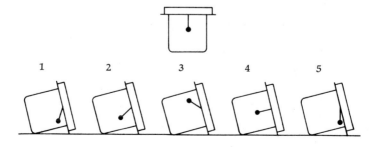

If the jar is tipped as shown, which figure shows the correct position of the string and marble?

    1. jar 1
    2. jar 2
    3. jar 3
    4. jar 4
    5. jar 5

20. Farmyards are constructed on two fields of the same size as shown below. Similar barns are placed on each field, but are arranged differently.

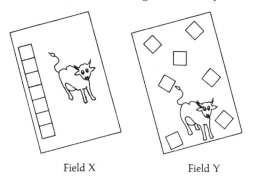

        Field X   Field Y

Compare the amount of grass that the cows will have to eat. Which of these statements is true?

    1. The cow in field X has more grass.
    2. The cow in field Y has more grass.
    3. Both cows have the same amount of grass.
    4. Impossible to say.

21. In the picture below, there are dark and light wild flowers.

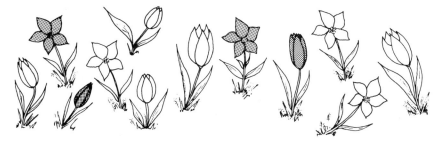

Are there more wild flowers than dark flowers?

    1. more wild flowers
    2. more dark flowers
    3. same number of wild flowers as dark flowers
    4. Impossible to say.

22. Two motorcycle riders are racing each other in a field toward a small bush. They start at the same time and arrive at the bush at the same time. The rider on the first cycle followed the path shown by the solid line, while the second cycle moved along the path shown by the dashes.

Bush

START

They end in a tie.

Compare the speeds of the two riders.

 1. The rider on the path shown by the solid line had a higher speed.
 2. The rider on the path shown by the dashes had a higher speed.
 3. The two riders had equal speeds.
 4. Impossible to say.

23. The cook has two pieces of cookie dough of the same size and weight. With one piece of dough she makes a boy cookie, and with the other piece she makes a football cookie.

Which of these statements is true?

 1. The boy cookie and the football cookie weigh the *same.*
 2. The boy cookie weighs *more* than the football cookie.
 3. The football cookie weighs *more* than the boy cookie.
 4. Impossible to say.

24. Linda and Cindy are going to paint the shapes drawn in the following boxes. Linda will paint the shapes in the box on the left and Cindy will paint those on the right.

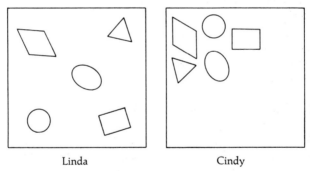

    Linda   Cindy

Which of these statements is true?

 1. Linda will have to do more painting.
 2. Cindy will have to do more painting.
 3. Linda and Cindy will do the same amount of painting.
 4. Impossible to say.

25. A newspaper has been crumpled up into a ball and thrown on the floor, as shown below. Does the crumpled newspaper weigh more, the same, or less than it did before it was crumpled?

1. It weighs the same.
2. It weighs less.
3. It weighs more.
4. Impossible to say.

26. A person using two different kinds of matches builds two roads as shown following.

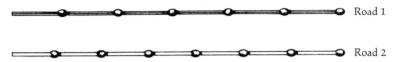

Suppose road 1 is left just as it is, while road 2 is changed into a zigzag pattern, as shown below.

Which of these statements is true for an ant walking from end to end after road 2 is changed?
    1. Road 1 is longer for the ant.
    2. Road 2 is longer for the ant.
    3. Road 1 and 2 are the same length for the ant.
    4. Impossible to say.

27. Susan is taller than Mary. Mark is shorter than Mary.

    Which of these statements is true?
    1. Susan is taller than Mark.
    2. Mark is the same height as Susan.
    3. Mark is taller than Susan.
    4. Mary is taller than Susan.

28. With a train set a boy sets the tracks as shown in Figure A. Next, using all of the same sections of track, he sets them as shown in Figure B.

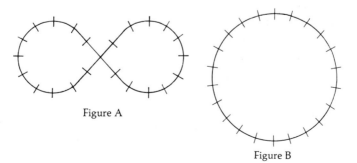

Figure A

Figure B

Which of these statements is true?

1. The train will have a longer trip around the track in Figure A.
2. The train will have a longer trip around the track in Figure B.
3. The length of the trip is the same on both sets of tracks.
4. Impossible to say.

29. John has two colored balls of clay, one dark and one light. The balls weigh the same. He separates the dark ball into three small balls, and flattens the light colored ball.

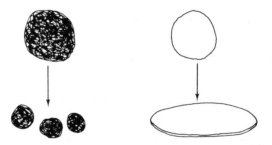

Which of these statements is true?

1. The three balls weigh more than the pancake.
2. The pancake weighs more than the three small balls.
3. The pancake weighs the same as the three small balls.
4. Impossible to say.

30. Two cars, called *Betsy* and *Jane,* are travelling along two roads side by side. In twenty minutes, Betsy goes six miles. In forty minutes, Jane travels ten miles. The figure following describes the distance each car travelled.

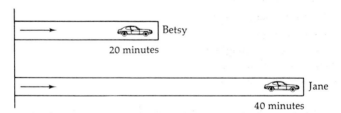

Which of these statements is true?

1. Betsy has a higher speed.
2. Jane has a higher speed.
3. The speeds of the two cars are equal.
4. Impossible to say.

Appendix B
Logical Reasoning Test

Directions: 1. For most of the questions on this test you will need only to place a cross (X) in the space on the answer sheet on page 172. For a few of the questions, you will be asked to give two or three answers. Instructions for answering these questions will be given when they appear in the test.

2. Several questions refer to diagrams and you should examine these diagrams closely before answering these questions.

3. If you have to change an answer, erase it completely and mark the new choice.

4. Try to answer all questions; if you are not sure of an answer, then choose the one that you think is most apt to be right.

5. Think carefully before you answer each question.

1. In the diagram following, the line XYZ represents a wall. A ball is thrown at the wall so that it always hits at point Y. Angle 1 equals angle 6, angle 2 equals angle 5, and angle 3 equals angle 4.

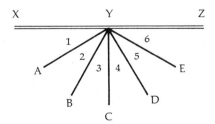

If a ball bounces from point Y to point B it must have been thrown from:

(a) A   (b) B   (c) C   (d) D   (e) E

Prepared by Gilbert M. Burney. From "The Construction and Validation of an Objective Formal Reasoning Instrument" (Ph.D. diss., University of Northern Colorado, 1974).

Here is a new diagram similar to the first one. Study it carefully and *use it to answer questions 2 and 3.*

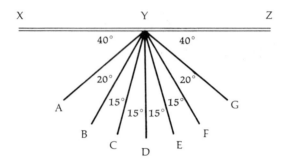

2. If a ball is thrown from point B to point Y on the wall, it will bounce to:
   (a) A   (b) E   (c) C   (d) F   (e) G

3. If a ball bounces from point Y on the wall to point A it must have been thrown from:
   (a) A   (b) E   (c) C   (d) F   (e) G

4. In the diagram below, a ball is thrown from point A to point Y on the wall.

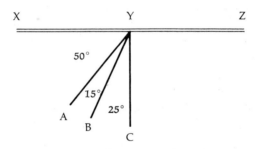

The angle the return path of the ball makes with CY is:
   (a) 50°   (b) 75°   (c) 65°   (d) 40°   (e) 25°

5. A ball is thrown from somewhere in the section marked *Right Side* in the diagram following. The ball hits the wall at point Y and bounces to point C.

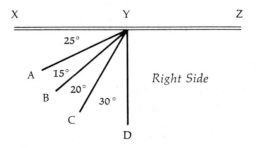

The size of the angle from YZ, the point from which the ball must be thrown, is:

(a) 25°   (b) 40°   (c) 65°   (d) 60°   (e) 50°

Suppose you have a balance scale similar to the one in the diagram following. Study the diagram carefully; answer questions 6–7.

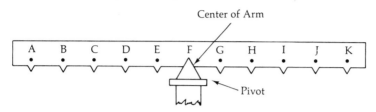

Weights which can be used:

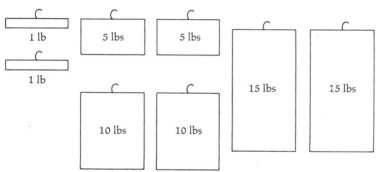

6. A five pound weight is hung at point D. How can you balance the arm?

   (a) Hang a one pound weight at A.
   (b) Hang a ten pound weight at J.
   (c) Hang a five pound weight at H.
   (d) Hang a ten pound weight at E.
   (e) Hang a five pound weight at K.
   (f) It is impossible.

7. A five pound weight is hung at point E and a ten pound weight at point C. How can you balance the arm?

   (a) Hang a five pound weight at G and a ten pound weight at J.
   (b) Hang a ten pound weight at H and a one pound weight at K.
   (c) Hang a fifteen pound weight at I and a one pound weight at H.
   (d) Hang a ten pound weight at I and a five pound weight at G.
   (e) It is impossible.
   (f) Hang a five pound weight at I and a ten pound weight at G.

Questions 8–10 are called *syllogisms*. Each syllogism consists of two premises and a conclusion. You are to determine whether each conclusion is valid or not.

Example:

P_1: No one-year-old babies can walk.

P_2: Paul is a one-year-old baby.

C: Paul cannot walk.

This is a valid conclusion.

8. P_1: Not all R's are T's.

   P_2: All T's are M's.

C: Some R's may not be M's.

(a) True   (b) False

9. P_1: All coal is white.

   P_2: All white coal produces red smoke when burning.

C: Therefore when coal burns, the smoke is grey.

(a) True   (b) False

10. P_1: When John gets angry at Mary he hits her.

    P_2: John is not angry at Mary.

C. Therefore John will not hit Mary.

(a) True   (b) False

The diagram following represents two open-top containers with water in them. There is a length of hose connecting them that will allow water to pass from one container to the other. Container B has a larger diameter than container A. Use the diagram to answer questions 11 and 12.

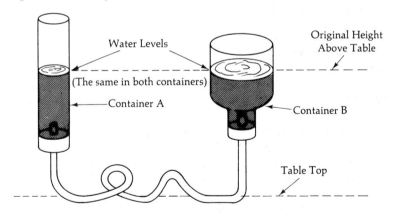

11. Container A and container B are moved down an equal distance. What will the water levels in the containers do?

(a) stay at the original height above the table

(b) change so that the level in A is above the original height and the level in B is below the original height

(c) change so that the level in B is above the original height and the level in A is below the original height

(d) change so that the levels in *A* and *B* are the same distance above the original height

(e) change so that the levels in *A* and *B* are the same distance below the original height

12. Container *A* and container *B* are moved up an equal distance. What will the water levels in the containers do?

   (a) stay at the original height above the table
   (b) change so that the levels in *A* and *B* are the same distance below the original height
   (c) change so that the level in *A* is above the original height and the level in *B* is below the original height
   (d) change so that the levels in *A* and *B* are the same distance above the original height
   (e) change so that the level in *B* is above the original height and the level in *A* is below the original height

The apparatus following can be used to throw shadows onto a screen. The rings pictured can be placed at points *D*, *E*, *F* or anywhere along lines through each of the three points between the light and screen. The shadows that are referred to in the questions are the circular shadows of the rings only, not the ring stands. The distances of points *D*, *E*, and *F* from the screen are indicated above and the distances of points *D*, *E*, and *F* from the light are indicated below the apparatus. Study the diagram carefully and use it to answer questions 13–14.

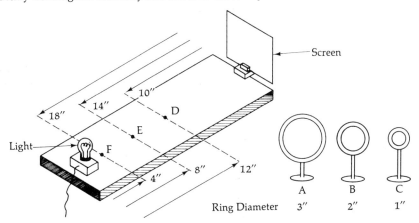

13. Ring *A* is placed at point *D* and when its shadow falls onto the screen the size of its shadow is measured. Ring *A* is removed and ring *B* is placed at *D*. The size of *B*'s shadow is measured. The two shadows formed:

   (a) will be of equal size.
   (b) will be of unequal size, the shadow of *A* being larger than the shadow of *B*.
   (c) will be of unequal size, the shadow of *B* being larger than the shadow of *A*.
   (d) will be of unequal size, the shadow of *A* being smaller than the shadow of *B*.

14. Ring *B* is placed at point *D* and when its shadow falls onto the screen the size of its shadow is measured. Ring *B* is removed and ring *C* is placed at D. The size of *C*'s shadow on the screen is measured. The two shadows formed:

(a) will be of equal size.
(b) will be of unequal size, the shadow of B being larger than the shadow of C.
(c) will be of unequal size, the shadow of C being larger than the shadow of B.
(d) will be of unequal size, the shadow of B being smaller than the shadow of C.

The diagram following represents two glasses (a small one and a large one) and two jars (a small one and a large one). Use this diagram for question 15.

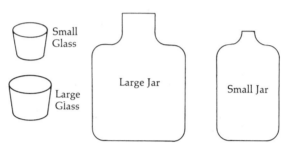

15. If it takes six large glasses of water or nine small glasses of water to fill the small jar, and it takes eight larges glasses of water to fill the large jar, then how many small glasses of water does it take to fill the large jar?

(a) 10   (b) 15   (c) 11   (d) 16   (e) 12

Questions 16–21 are called *verbal analogies*. Verbal analogies consist of two pairs of words, each pair having the same relationship. For example, *in* is to *out* as *up* is to *down*. The common relationship between *in–out* and *up–down* is that they are opposites. Order of the pair of words is also important. Although *peel* is to *banana* as *paint* is to *house* is correct, *peel* is to *banana* as *house* is to *paint* is incorrect. In the following questions you are to choose two or three words that will best complete each analogy. Some questions require two answers and some require three.

Example:

(a) tire   (e) anchor
(b) motor   (f) deck
(c) highway   is to *car*   as   (g) captain   is to *ship*
(d) map   (h) ocean

In this example, the best choices to complete the analogy are *highway* and *ocean* resulting in the analogy: *Highway* is to *car* as *ocean* is to *ship*. In this case *operates on* is the common relationship; a car operates on a highway and a ship operates on the ocean. On the answer sheet the above question would be answered as shown below.

a   b   c   d   e   f   g   h
( )   ( )   (X)   ( )   ( )   ( )   ( )   (X)

Be careful to mark all required answers for each question on the answer sheet.

(a) attempt   (e) problem
(b) completion   (f) chemical
16. *task* is to (c) work   as   (g) man   is to *solution*
(d) question   (h) answer

17. *light bulb* is to
   (a) switch
   (b) wire
   (c) socket
   (d) electricity
as
   (e) engine
   (f) canoe
   (g) motor
   (h) steam
is to
   (i) boat
   (j) engine
   (k) tractor
   (l) paddle

18.
   (a) walk
   (b) toe
   (c) knee
   (d) foot
is to *body* as *wheel* is to
   (e) roll
   (f) machine
   (g) bicycle
   (h) spokes

19.
   (a) cow
   (b) horse
   (c) sheep
   (d) foot
is to *flock* as
   (e) soldier
   (f) swarm
   (g) pack
   (h) litter
is to
   (i) bee
   (j) pig
   (k) regiment
   (l) wolf

20.
   (a) brain
   (b) eye
   (c) hat
   (d) ear
is to *head* as
   (e) spring
   (f) blanket
   (g) caster
   (h) pillow
is to
   (i) bedpost
   (j) ticking
   (k) bed
   (l) summer

21.
   (a) music
   (b) house
   (c) bench
   (d) tuner
is to *piano* as
   (e) chair
   (f) leg
   (g) eat
   (h) furniture
is to *table*

Logical Reasoning
Answer Sheet

1.	a	b	c	d	e	
	( )	( )	( )	( )	( )	

Name_____

Date of birth

_____month _____day _____year

Year in school_____

2.	a	b	c	d	e						
	( )	( )	( )	( )	( )						
3.	a	b	c	d	e						
	( )	( )	( )	( )	( )						
4.	a	b	c	d	e						
	( )	( )	( )	( )	( )						
5.	a	b	c	d	e						
	( )	( )	( )	( )	( )						
6.	a	b	c	d	e	f					
	( )	( )	( )	( )	( )	( )					
7.	a	b	c	d	e	f					
	( )	( )	( )	( )	( )	( )					
8.	a	b									
	( )	( )									
9.	a	b									
	( )	( )									
10.	a	b									
	( )	( )									
11.	a	b	c	d	e						
	( )	( )	( )	( )	( )						
12.	a	b	c	d	e						
	( )	( )	( )	( )	( )						
13.	a	b	c	d							
	( )	( )	( )	( )							
14.	a	b	c	d							
	( )	( )	( )	( )							
15.	a	b	c	d	e						
	( )	( )	( )	( )	( )						
16.	a	b	c	d	e	f	g	h			
	( )	( )	( )	( )	( )	( )	( )	( )			
17.	a	b	c	d	e	f	g	h	i	j	k	l
	( )	( )	( )	( )	( )	( )	( )	( )	( )	( )	( )	( )
18.	a	b	c	d	e	f	g	h			
	( )	( )	( )	( )	( )	( )	( )	( )			
19.	a	b	c	d	e	f	g	h	i	j	k	l
	( )	( )	( )	( )	( )	( )	( )	( )	( )	( )	( )	( )
20.	a	b	c	d	e	f	g	h	i	j	k	l
	( )	( )	( )	( )	( )	( )	( )	( )	( )	( )	( )	( )
21.	a	b	c	d	e	f	g	h			
	( )	( )	( )	( )	( )	( )	( )	( )			

Logical Reasoning
Answer Sheet

	a	b	c	d	e		Name __KEY__
1.	( )	( )	( )	(X)	( )		Date of birth

	a	b	c	d	e	
2.	( )	( )	( )	(X)	( )	____month ____day ____year

Year in school_____

	a	b	c	d	e	
3.	( )	( )	( )	( )	(X)	In order to be counted correct, questions
4.	( )	( )	( )	(X)	( )	16–21 must be marked exactly as they
	a	b	c	d	e	are marked on the key.

	a	b	c	d	e	
5.	( )	( )	( )	(X)	( )	

RATING

	a	b	c	d	e	f	
6.	( )	( )	(X)	( )	( )	( )	Formal 14–21

Transitional 8–13

	a	b	c	d	e	f	
7.	( )	( )	( )	(X)	( )	( )	Concrete or below 0–7

	a	b
8.	(X)	( )
9.	( )	(X)
10.	( )	(X)

	a	b	c	d	e
11.	( )	( )	( )	( )	(X)
12.	( )	( )	( )	(X)	( )

	a	b	c	d
13.	( )	(X)	( )	( )
14.	( )	(X)	( )	( )

	a	b	c	d	e
15.	( )	( )	( )	( )	(X)

	a	b	c	d	e	f	g	h
16.	( )	(X)	( )	( )	(X)	( )	( )	( )

	a	b	c	d	e	f	g	h	i	j	k	l
17.	( )	( )	( )	(X)	( )	(X)	( )	( )	( )	( )	( )	(X)

	a	b	c	d	e	f	g	h
18.	( )	( )	( )	(X)	( )	( )	(X)	( )

	a	b	c	d	e	f	g	h	i	j	k	l
19.	( )	( )	(X)	( )	(X)	( )	( )	( )	( )	( )	(X)	( )
20.	( )	( )	(X)	( )	( )	(X)	( )	( )	( )	( )	(X)	( )

	a	b	c	d	e	f	g	h
21.	( )	( )	(X)	( )	(X)	( )	( )	( )

Appendix C
Recommended Films
and Filmstrips

Today there are excellent films describing aspects of Piaget's theory. In these films children are interviewed at various stages of development. Following is a list of films giving pertinent information about each. It is strongly recommended that you see them in the order given below. If you really want to become proficient in applying Piaget's theory and developing good interviewing techniques, view the films several times.[1]

Conservation—28 minutes, $360

Children between the ages of five and twelve are presented in individual interviews involving tasks using standard procedures developed by Piaget. The tasks involve conservation of quantity, length, area, and volume. The characteristics of thought from preoperational to formal are identified.

Classification—17 minutes, $200

Children are shown at several developmental stages responding to tasks that highlight mental operations essential to classification, such as multiple classification, class inclusion, and hierarchical classification.

Formal Thought—32 minutes, $400

This film illustrates tasks that challenge the thinking of secondary school students. The tasks involve proportional reasoning, separation of variables, combinatorial logic and the integration of these in an analysis of a balance beam with weights.

The Growth of Intelligence in the Preschool Years—31¼ minutes, $390

The growth of thinking processes in the preschool years is the basis for this film. Children from three to six years of age are presented with tasks which reveal how they are thinking as they sort objects, put them in one-to-one correspondence or arrange them in order of size. The interview material is used not only to illustrate development changes, but also to clarify certain Piagetian terms.

---

[1] Film descriptions prepared by Davidson Films, 1757 Union St., San Francisco, Calif. 94123.

Jean Piaget—Memory and Intelligence—45 minutes, $450

A filmed documentary of Jean Piaget presenting his new work on memory and intelligence at the International Congress of Preschool Educational Specialists in Kyoto, Japan. Carefully translated English subtitles accompany Piaget's presentation in French. The film affords the opportunity to experience the presence of Jean Piaget.

Filmstrip and Record Program

Celia Stendler Lavatelli has prepared a Piaget-oriented curriculum for children in preschool and the lower primary grades. It consists of curriculum materials, a teacher's guide, and two teacher-training filmstrips and records (or cassettes). The curriculum materials and guide are available from:

A Center for Media Development
American Science and Engineering, Inc.,
20 Overland Street, Boston, Mass. 02215

The two teacher-training items are:
Piaget Preschool Program—records $45.00
Piaget Preschool Program—cassettes $48.00

and are available from: Knowledge Tree Films
Box 203
Little Neck, New York 11363

Audio-Tapes

David Elkind has produced four audio-tapes explaining Piaget's theory. They are entitled "History and Application," "Implications for Curriculum Structure," "Piaget's Theory of Learning," and "Applications for Teachers and Teaching." The set of four tapes may be purchased from:

Listener Educational Enterprises
6777 Hollywood Blvd.
Hollywood, California 90028

Appendix D
Final Self-evaluation
Inventory

Directions: Listed below are the objectives relative to Piaget's theory, which you have been studying. Read each statement and rate it on the scale TWICE: once according to what you knew about the topic before studying this theory and again according to what you have learned after completing this portion of your study. Circle the appropriate number and mark B for before and A for after next to it, as indicated below.

Topic	Student Evaluation		
	Low	Moderate	High
Example: Important Piagetian mental operations.	1 ②B 3	4	⑤A 6

Topic	Low		Moderate		High	
1. State the four stages of Piaget's developmental theory and their age spans.	1	2	3	4	5	6
2. Identify five characteristics of each of the stages.	1	2	3	4	5	6
3. Define these terms: conservation of area, weight, volume	1	2	3	4	5	6
formal reasoning	1	2	3	4	5	6
reversibility	1	2	3	4	5	6
class inclusion	1	2	3	4	5	6
class hierarchy	1	2	3	4	5	6
pseudo-learning	1	2	3	4	5	6

	1	2	3	4	5	6
equilibration	1	2	3	4	5	6
assimilation	1	2	3	4	5	6
accommodation	1	2	3	4	5	6
scheme	1	2	3	4	5	6
auto-regulation	1	2	3	4	5	6
propositional thought	1	2	3	4	5	6
reflexive thinking	1	2	3	4	5	6
hypothetical-deductive thinking	1	2	3	4	5	6
combinatorial logic	1	2	3	4	5	6
theoretical thinking	1	2	3	4	5	6
syllogistic reasoning	1	2	3	4	5	6
representational thought	1	2	3	4	5	6
object permanence	1	2	3	4	5	6
egocentricity	1	2	3	4	5	6
operations	1	2	3	4	5	6
perception bound	1	2	3	4	5	6
4. The characteristics of each of the six sensory-motor stages	1	2	3	4	5	6
5. The three types of memory and their characteristics	1	2	3	4	5	6
6. Three Piagetian moral levels and their characteristics	1	2	3	4	5	6
7. Kohlberg's six levels and their characteristics	1	2	3	4	5	6
8. The Jean Jacques Rosseau Institute and its work	1	2	3	4	5	6
9. The contributions of Barbel Inhelder to the work of the institute	1	2	3	4	5	6
10. The four factors contributing to intelligence and their role	1	2	3	4	5	6

11. The importance of action in the equilibration process	1	2	3	4	5	6
12. The relationship of object permanence and identity	1	2	3	4	5	6
13. The significance of Piaget's theory for reading	1	2	3	4	5	6
14. Ten educational implications of Piaget's theory	1	2	3	4	5	6
15. Two reasons for having students learn by discovery	1	2	3	4	5	6
16. Indicate that having learned about Piaget's theory affects the way you look at students.	1	2	3	4	5	6
17. Indicate the value of this Piagetian program.	1	2	3	4	5	6
18. Indicate that you would like to learn more about Piaget's work.	1	2	3	4	5	6

Appendix E
An Introductory
Piagetian Bibliography

Almy, Millie; Chittenden, E.; and Miller, P. *Young Children's Thinking: Studies of Some Aspects of Piaget's Theory.* New York: Teachers College Press, 1966.

Beard, Ruth M. *An Outline of Piaget's Developmental Psychology for Students and Teachers.* New York: Basic Books, 1969.

Brearley, Molly, and Hitchfield, Elizabeth. *A Guide to Reading Piaget.* New York: Schocken Books, 1966.

Bruner, Jerome S. *Process of Education.* New York: Vintage, 1960.

Copeland, Richard W. *How Children Learn Mathematics, Teaching Implications of Piaget's Research.* New York: Macmillan, 1974.

Duckworth, Eleanor. "Piaget Rediscovered." *Journal of Research in Science Teaching* 2 (1964): 172–75.

Elkind, David, and Flavell, J. H. *Studies in Cognitive Development, Essays in Honor of Jean Piaget.* New York: Oxford University, 1969.

* Elkind, David, "Children and Adolescents, Interpretive Essays of Jean Piaget," New York: Oxford University, 1974.

Elkind, David. "Quantity Conceptions and Senior High School Students," *Child Development* 32 (1961): 551–60.

† Flavell, John H. *The Developmental Psychology of Jean Piaget.* Princeton: D. Van Nostrand, 1963.

* Furth, Hans, and Wachs, Harry. *Piaget's Theory in Practice, Thinking Goes to School.* New York: Oxford University, 1974.

Furth, Hans. *Piaget for Teachers.* Englewood Cliffs, N.J.: Prentice-Hall, 1970.

* Ginsberg, Herbert, and Opper, Sylvia. *Piaget's Theory of Intellectual Development.* Englewood Cliffs, N.J.: Prentice-Hall, 1969.

* Gorman, Richard M. *Discovering Piaget: A Guide for Teachers.* Columbus, Ohio: Charles E. Merrill, 1972.

---

* Good book to begin with for any study of Piaget.
† Most complete work on Piaget.

Inhelder, B. and Piaget, J. *The Early Growth of Logic in the Child.* New York: Norton, 1964.

Lavatelli, Stendler Celia. *Piaget's Theory Applied to Early Childhood Curriculum.* Boston: Center for Media Development, American Science and Engineering, 1970.

Lubin, Gerald I.; Magary, James F.; and Poulsen, Marie K. *Piagetian Theory and the Helping Professions.* Los Angeles, California: Publication Department, University of Southern California, 1975.

Maier, Henry W. *Three Theories of Child Development.* New York: Harper and Row, 1965.

*Phillips, J. L., Jr. *The Origins of Intellect: Piaget's Theory.* San Francisco: W. H. Freeman, 1969.

Piaget, Jean. "Development and Learning." *Journal of Research in Science Teaching* 2 (1964): 176–86.

———. *Six Psychological Studies.* Edited by David Elkind. New York: Random House, 1967.

Piaget, Jean, *Science of Education and the Psychology of the Child.* New York: Orion, 1970.

Piaget, Jean, and Inhelder, Barbel. *The Psychology of the Child.* New York: Basic Books, 1969.

*Pulaski, Mary Ann Spencer. *Understanding Piaget.* New York: Harper & Row, 1971.

Ripple, Richard E., and Rockcastle, Verne N., eds. *Piaget Rediscovered.* New York: Cornell University, School of Education, 1964. Also entire conference proceeding reported in *Journal of Research in Science Teaching* 2 (3) (1964).

Rosskopf, Myron; Steffe, Leslie P.; and Taback, Stanley, eds. *Piagetian Cognitive Development Research and Mathematical Education.* Washington, D.C.: NCTM, 1971.

Stendler, Celia B., "Elementary Teaching and Piagetian Theory." *The Science Teacher* 29 (September, 1962): 34.

Sullivan, Edmund V. *Piaget and the School Curriculum—A Critical Appraisal.* Ontario: Ontario Institute for Studies in Education, 1967. Bull. 2.

*Wadsworth, Barry. *Piaget's Theory of Cognitive Development, An Introduction for Students of Psychology and Education.* N.Y.: David McKay, 1972.

* Good book to begin with for any study of Piaget.
† Most complete work on Piaget.

Index

Abstract reasoning, in formal operations, 49, 75

Accommodation, and equilibrium, 7–8

Action, and perceptual ability, 81

Action representation, in concrete operations, 46

Adults
 and the child's mind, 58
 as influential, 60–62

Allegory, comprehending, 51

Almy, Millie, 63, 77, 80

Animism
 concrete-operational activity, 142
 preoperational activity, 132

Animistic explanation, 27

Art, preoperational activity for, 128–29

Artificialism activities
 concrete-operational, 142
 preoperational, 131–32

Artificialistic explanation, in preoperational stage, 27–28

Ascending hierarchy, in concrete operation, 45, 140

Assimilation, and equilibration, 7–8

Assumptions, accepting, 51

Authority
 and moral development, 85, 101
 questioning and accepting, 53

Ball, Daniel W., 76, 77, 79, 80

Binet, Alfred, 2

Biological Sciences Curriculum Study (BSCS), 71, 74

Biology, value clarification example, 113

Bruner, Jerome, 65, 70, 71, 74, 91

Change, relating, in preoperational activity, 128

Child's mind, 58–60

Classification
 in concrete-operational stage, 38, 43
  ascending and descending hierarchy, 140
  sequence, 44–45
 in formal operations, 53
 preoperational activity, 122

Class inclusion
 concrete-operational activity, 143
 preoperational activity, 123

Cognitive ability, levels of, and ethical development, 105

Cognitive achievements
 in concrete-operational stage, 46
 in formal-operational stage, 55
 in preoperational stage, 34
 in sensory-motor stage, 21–22

Cognitive development
 concepts of, for teaching, 88
 four stages, 5–6
  descriptions of, 9–12
 influences on
  equilibration, 7–9
  maturation and experience, 6
  social experience, 6
 psychological factors, 4

College students, and formal tasks, 79, 80

Combinatorial logic, in formal-operational period, 52, 146–47

Concrete-operational stage, 5, 38–47
 description of, 11
 interview activities for, 136–43
 a summary of, 12
 teaching suggestions for, 93
 transition activities, 136, 140–42

Concrete operations, in BSCS curriculum, 74–75

Conflict, in value clarification, 108–9

Conflict strategies, 90

Conservation
 in concrete-operational stage, 39–41
  activity for, 140
 formal-operational activity, 150
 in preoperational stage, 31–32
  activities, 123–25, 130

Curriculum
 early childhood, 73
 elementary science, 73
 teaching suggestions for, 89–91

Curriculum planning, 71
 information needed, 72

Correspondence, concrete-operational activity, 137–38

Counting, in concrete operations, 42–43

Darwin, Charles, 4

Deductive reasoning (thinking)
 formal-operational activity, 148
 hypothetical, 97

181

Limited hypotheses, in concrete operations, 45–46

Logic
  combinatorial, 52, 146–47
  semi, 30–31

Logical and infralogical operations, 23–24

Logical-mathematical experience, 6, 28–29

Logical reasoning, memory, formal-operational activity, 149–50

Lovell, Kenneth, 71, 78

McCluhan, Marshall, 63

McKinnon, Joe W., 79, 80

McREL Inquiry Role, 96

Maslow, Abraham, 3, 5

Mathematical operations, in concrete operations, 38, 41–42

Maturation, and cognitive development, 6, 8

Measurement, and preoperational stage, 32

Memorizing vs. reasoning, 58–59

Memory logical reasoning, formal-operational activity, 149–50

Memory task, for preoperational activities, 135

Mental actions, in concrete operations, 46

Mentally involved in learning, 90

Mental health, 82
  emotional problems, 83–84

Moral development, Piaget's stages, 101–2
  (*see also* Ethical development)

Morals, evolving with cognitive stages, 84–85

Motor training, and perceptual problems, 81–82

Number
  in concrete-operational stage, 40, 42–43
    activity for, 142
  in preoperational stage, 32
    activities for, 126–27

Object constancy, 32

Object permanence, 67
  and sensory-motor stage, 9, 19–20

One-to-one correspondence, in preoperational activity, 125–26

Ordering activities
  concrete-operational, 137
  preoperational, 134

Part-whole relationship, concrete-operational activity, 141

Perception
  grouping, in concrete operations, 44
  in preoperational stage, 33
    activity, 131

Perception-bound
  in preoperational stage, 32
    activities, 127–28

Perceptual problems, and motor training, 81–82

Performing operations period, concrete-operational stage, 11

Physical causality, concrete-operational activity, 142

Physical experience, 6, 8
  and preoperational stage, 28–29

Physically involved in learning, 90

Piagetian interviews. *See* Interviews

Piaget's theory
  caution in application of, 85–87
  the need to apply, 57

Play
  and preoperational stage, 29
  and sensory-motor stage, 21

Preoperational stage, 5, 23–37
  description of, 10
  interview activities for, 122–35
  teaching suggestions for, 92
  a summary of, 12

Problems, originating, 95

Propositional thinking, 97
  in formal-operational stage, 11, 50

Pseudo-learning, 89

Punishment, and ethical development, 102, 104

Quantity
  in concrete-operational stage, 40
  in preoperational stage, 32

Readiness, in learning, 65–66, 89

Reading, early emphasis on, 62–64

Realism, 26–28, 132

Reasoning (*see also* Thinking)
  in formal operations
    abstract, 49
    activities, 144, 145–46, 148–50
    syllogistic, 50
    varied, 54
  and memorizing, 58–59
  in preoperational stage, 29

Reflexive thinking, 51–52, 96

Relativist orientation, instrumental, 102

Renner, John W., 75, 79, 80

Reversing thinking
  in concrete-operational stage, 38, 139
  in preoperational stage, 26, 134

Role playing, 90

Russell, Bertrand, 60

Sayre, Steve A., 76, 77, 79, 80

Schemes, and equilibration, 8

Schooling, early, 64

Schools, and ethical development, 106–8

Science—A Process Approach (SAPA), 73

Science curriculum, elementary, 73–75

Science Curriculum Improvement Study (SCIS), 71, 73, 74

Self-evaluation inventories, 14–15, 36, 98–100, 115–16

Semilogic, in preoperational stage, 31

Sensory-motor stage, 5, 16–22
  description of, 9–10
  a summary of, 11